William Mackenzie, Percy Handford

Model Byelaws, Rules and Regulations under the Public Health and other Acts

Vol. II

William Mackenzie, Percy Handford

Model Byelaws, Rules and Regulations under the Public Health and other Acts
Vol. II

ISBN/EAN: 9783337157586

Printed in Europe, USA, Canada, Australia, Japan

Cover: Foto ©ninafisch / pixelio.de

More available books at **www.hansebooks.com**

MODEL BYELAWS

RULES AND REGULATIONS

UNDER

THE PUBLIC HEALTH AND OTHER ACTS,

With Alternative and Additional Clauses,

PREPARED AND EDITED BY

WILLIAM MACKENZIE, M.A.,

Barrister-at-Law; Editor of "Pratt's Law of Highways," etc.

AND

PERCY HANDFORD,

Author of "Parish Councils," etc.

IN TWO VOLUMES.

VOL. II.

CONTAINING

SUPPLEMENTARY BYELAWS, RULES, AND REGULATIONS UNDER THE PUBLIC HEALTH AND OTHER ACTS.

LONDON:

SHAW & SONS, 7 & 8 FETTER LANE, E.C.

BUTTERWORTH & CO., 12, BELL YARD, TEMPLE BAR, W.C.

Law Printers and Publishers.

1899.

TABLE OF CONTENTS.

PART I.

STREETS AND BUILDINGS.

PART II.

TENT AND VAN DWELLINGS AND HOUSING OF HOP-PICKERS, FRUIT-PICKERS, AND OTHERS.

PART III.

PUBLIC FOOD SUPPLY.

PART IV.

PUBLIC CONVEYANCES.

PART V.

PUBLIC RECREATION.

PART VI.

SCAVENGING.

PART VII.

PUBLIC CONVENIENCES AND CABMEN'S SHELTERS.

PART VIII.

ALLOTMENTS.

TABLE OF STATUTES.

TABLE OF CASES.

MODEL BYELAWS.

PART I.

STREETS AND BUILDINGS.

NEW STREETS AND BUILDINGS, AND ALTERATION OF BUILDINGS.

MEMORANDUM.

Authority for the Byelaws.

Section 157 of the Public Health Act, 1875 (38 & 39 Vict. c. 55), authorises (according to the Revised Statutes) the making, by any Urban Authority, of byelaws as to the following matters, viz.:

"(1.) With respect to the level width and construction of new streets, and the provisions for the sewerage thereof:

"(2.) With respect to the structure of walls, foundations, roofs, and chimneys of new buildings, for securing stability and the prevention of fires, and for purposes of health:

"(3.) With respect to the sufficiency of the space about buildings to secure a free circulation of air, and with respect to the ventilation of buildings:

"(4.) With respect to the drainage of buildings, to water-closets, earthclosets, privies, ashpits, and cesspools in connection with buildings, and to the closing of buildings or parts of buildings unfit for human habitation, and to prohibition of their use for such habitation,"

and it enables the authority to "provide for the observance of such byelaws by enacting therein such provisions as they think necessary as to the giving of notices, as to the deposit of plans and sections by persons intending to lay out streets or to construct buildings, as to inspection by the Urban Authority, and as to the power of such authority (subject to the provisions of this Act) to remove, alter, or pull down any work begun or done in contravention of such byelaws."

The section provides, however, that "no byelaw made under this section shall affect any building erected in any place (which at the time of the passing of this Act is included in an urban sanitary district) before the Local Government Acts came into force in such place, or any building erected in any place (which at the time of the passing of this Act is not included in an urban sanitary district) before such place becomes constituted or included in an urban district, or by virtue of any order of the Local Government Board subject to this enactment."

The provisions of this section do not apply to buildings belonging to any railway company and used for the purposes of such railway under any Act of Parliament.

Section 23 of the Public Health Acts Amendment Act, 1890 (53 & 54 Vict. c. 59), extends the above-mentioned enactment as follows:

"(1.) Section one hundred and fifty-seven of the Public Health Act, 1875, shall be extended so as to empower every urban authority to make byelaws with respect to the following matters; that is to say:—

"The keeping waterclosets supplied with sufficient water for flushing;

"The structure of floors, hearths, and staircases, and the height of rooms intended to be used for human habitation;

"The paving of yards and open spaces in connection with dwelling-houses; and

"The provision in connection with the laying out of new streets of secondary means of access where necessary for the purpose of the removal of house refuse and other matters.

"(2.) Any byelaws under that section as above extended with regard to the drainage of buildings, and to waterclosets, earthclosets, privies, ashpits, and cesspools, in connection with buildings, and the keeping waterclosets supplied with sufficient water for flushing, may be made so as to affect buildings erected before the times mentioned in the said section.

"(3.) The provisions of the said section (as amended by this Act), so far as they relate to byelaws with respect to the structure of walls and foundations of new buildings for purposes of health, and with respect to the matters mentioned in sub-sections (3) and (4) of the said section, and with respect to the structure of floors, the height of rooms to be used for human habitation, and to the keeping of waterclosets supplied with sufficient water for flushing, shall be extended so as to empower rural authorities to make byelaws in respect to the said matters, and to provide for the observance of such byelaws, and to enforce the same as if such powers were conferred on the rural authorities by virtue of an order of the Local Government Board made on the day when this part of this Act is adopted; and section one hundred and fifty-eight of the Public Health Act, 1875, shall also apply to any such authority, and shall be in force in every rural district where this part of this Act is adopted.

"(4.) Every local authority may make byelaws to prevent buildings which have been erected in accordance with byelaws made under the Public Health Acts from being altered in such a way that if at first so constructed they would have contravened the byelaws."

The effect of these provisions is,—

First, to enable any rural authority which has adopted Part III. of the Act of 1890 (see sections 3 and 50 of the Act) to make byelaws on the following subjects mentioned in section 157 of the Public Health Act, 1875, although otherwise that section refers only to urban authorities, viz.,—

(*a.*) The structure of walls and foundations of buildings for purposes of health;

(*b.*) Space about buildings, and the ventilation of buildings;

(*c.*) The drainage of buildings;

(*d.*) Waterclosets, earthclosets, privies, ashpits, and cesspools in connection with buildings; and

(*e.*) The closing of buildings unfit for human habitation.

Secondly, any local authority, whether urban or rural, may (if they have adopted Part III. of the Act of 1890), make byelaws on the following matters, which are *not* mentioned in section 157 of the Public Health Act, 1875, viz.,—

(*f.*) The structure of floors;

(*g.*) The height of rooms;

(*h.*) The flushing of waterclosets; and

(*i.*) The alteration of buildings.

Further, an urban authority may, after adopting Part III. of the Public Health Acts Amendment Act, 1890, make byelaws on certain other additional subjects, viz.,—

(*j*.) The structure of hearths and staircases;

(*k*.) The paving of yards; and

(*l*.) The provision of secondary means of access to buildings.

Lastly, any byelaws as to—

(i.) The drainage of buildings;

(ii.) Waterclosets, earthclosets, privies, ashpits, and cesspools in connection with buildings; and

(iii.) The flushing of waterclosets,

may be made so as to affect any building, whether erected before or after the times mentioned in section 157 of the Public Health Act, 1875.

Any part of section 23 of the Act of 1890 which is not in force in a rural district may be put in force therein by an order of the Local Government Board (section 5 of the Act).

Such byelaws as to the construction of roofs as are included in the present series can be made by any urban district council, and by any rural district council invested with the necessary "urban powers." The authority for these byelaws is section 157 (2) of the Public Health Act, 1875.

Scope of the Model Byelaws.

The annexed model byelaws are designed to supplement the series as to new streets and buildings, issued by the Local Government Board in the year 1877, in such a way as to enable local authorities to take the fullest practicable advantage of the powers conferred by section 23 of the Public Health Acts Amendment Act, 1890. The only matter germane to the subject which is not dealt with in the series is the extension to old buildings of any byelaws which may have been or may be made by the local authority with respect to drainage. (See sub-sections (2) (3) of section 23 of the Act.) It may, however, be questioned whether it is practicable to deal with this matter by means of byelaws. The omission of some provisions which might otherwise have been inserted in the clauses with respect to the structure of roofs, floors, and staircases, is due to considerations of a similar nature. Great care, however, has been taken to provide as to all such matters as can usefully be made the subject of byelaws, and it is believed that the series, as a whole, is more complete than any which has yet been suggested, or which has come into force anywhere in the kingdom, under the statutory enactments above mentioned. As to some other of the suggested clauses the following observations may be offered.

Secondary means of access.

Section 23 of the Public Health Acts Amendment Act, 1890, provides for the making of byelaws on this subject in connection only with the laying out of new streets; and the byelaws can only apply where secondary means of access are "necessary for the purpose of the removal of house refuse *and* other matters." But there is nothing to prevent the local authority so framing their byelaws as to specify certain kinds of "other matters," as suggested in clause 3 of this series. It should be borne in mind that secondary means of access may be given without necessarily providing "back streets." But the width of secondary access streets is best regulated by adopting a model clause (6 A.) of which copies may be obtained from the Local Government Board: it is scarcely within the scope of the present series.

Timbers of roofs and floors.

The framing of byelaws prescribing scantlings for timbers of roofs and floors is, for various reasons, a matter of some difficulty. It is believed, however, that the clauses contained in the present series will be found to be sufficiently elastic in their application to obviate any objection on the ground of undue stringency, while, at the same time, proper stability is secured. Attention may be directed to the regulations contained in the provisoes to clauses 4 and 8, and elsewhere in the series. The model series should, as regards the strength of timbers, be treated as suggesting what may be termed the mean, rather than the maximum, or even the minimum requirements under this head. The object which has been kept in view in the preparation of the series, has been to afford to local authorities proposing to regulate the structure of roofs and floors, a safe guide as to the provisions which they may reasonably embody in their byelaws. Some regard must be paid to local practice in these matters, but if it is found necessary to modify the requirements of the model byelaws, the modifications should be well considered, so as not to affect stability of structure. The rigidity of the timbers, as well as their bearing strength, is a matter to be considered if such modifications are proposed.

Height of rooms.

The model byelaw which has been framed on this subject prescribes conditions which should be fulfilled in the case of every room which is intended for human habitation. The chief value of such a clause consists in its application to attic rooms where, as regards air-space and ventilation, insanitary conditions are more likely to prevail than in rooms which are constructed with flat ceilings. The aim here should be to secure an average height of not less than *eight feet* over the entire area of the floor; and this should be obtained without the ceiling being allowed to slant away in any part of the room to less than *five feet* from the floor. The byelaw, as framed, gives an average height of *eight feet four inches* for such rooms.

Paving of yards.

The first of the two clauses on this subject is applicable more particularly to existing, and the second to new houses. The local authority are recommended to adopt both.

Flushing of waterclosets.

The byelaw in this case is framed so as to apply to the occupier, rather than the owner, because the flushing of waterclosets is a matter requiring constant attention, and the owner would not be on the spot to perform the duty. The provision of flushing *apparatus* will be secured and regulated, where the model byelaws of the Local Government Board are in force by clause 69 of that series: the matter is beyond the scope of byelaws under section 23 of the Public Health Acts Amendment Act, 1890, and, it may be added, there is no authority in that section for a byelaw requiring a supply of water to be laid on for flushing purposes.

Alteration of buildings.

Clause 21 of this series, and the subsidiary clauses as to the giving of notices, deposit of plans, etc., follow closely the terms of the enactment authorising the byelaws. No attempt should be made to define by the byelaws what will constitute a "new building," and what may be regarded merely as an "alteration" of a building. This is a question to be decided in the first instance, if necessary, by the justices, in connection with any proceedings that may be taken to enforce the byelaws. Reference may be made, however, to the provisions of section 159 of the Public Health Act, 1875. If, of course, the "alterations" are of such a nature as to constitute a new building, the person making the alterations may be subject to more recent byelaws than those in accordance with which the building was originally erected; and this is important when the effect of section 326 of the Public Health Act, 1875, is borne in mind. It will be seen that byelaws made long before 1875 may be "byelaws made under the Public Health Acts," within the meaning of section 23 (4) of the Act of 1890.

Giving of notices, deposit of plans and sections, etc.

It is assumed that clauses similar to the Local Government Board's model byelaws as to these matters (numbers 91 to 97 in Series IV., both inclusive) have been, or will be adopted by the local authority. An additional clause (No. 20) is suggested in connection with the requirements of clause 3 of the present series, and to this are added clauses applicable to the alteration of buildings. The power to provide for the observance of byelaws under section 23 (4) of the Public Health Acts Amendment Act, 1890, by enacting therein such provisions as are necessary with regard to the giving of notices, etc., may be inferred from the fact that the whole of the section (including sub-section (4)) is treated by the Act as an "extension" of section 157 of the Act of 1875, which authorises the enactment of such provisions.

Arrangement of the clauses.

As in many cases local authorities may wish to combine the present series with the model clauses as to new streets and buildings issued by the Local Government Board, it has been thought convenient to indicate the place which the clauses under each sub-heading should occupy in such a combined series. The letter "M" has been used to denote the number of the clause of the Local Government Board, after which any clause or group of clauses should be placed. The clause as to the removal, alteration, etc., of work done contrary to the byelaws, should not be made to apply to the clauses as to the alteration of buildings, notwithstanding what is stated in the note above. The power to make byelaws under section 157 of the Public Health Act, 1875, embodying provisions as to the power of the Council to remove, alter, or pull down any work begun or done in contravention of such byelaws, is made subject to the provisions of section 158 of that Act; and the provisions of the latter section are not extended so as to apply to the alteration of buildings. The numbers inserted in clause 28 may require alteration. As they stand, they refer to the clauses in the present series only.

Confirmation of the Byelaws.

Byelaws made under section 23 of the Public Health Acts Amendment Act, 1890, require confirmation by the Local Government Board, to whom a draft of any proposed clauses should be submitted before any formal steps are taken with regard to the adoption of the byelaws. For this purpose, appropriate draft forms have been issued by the publishers of the present work.

NEW STREETS AND BUILDINGS AND ALTERATION OF BUILDINGS.

BYELAWS

MADE BY THE* WITH RESPECT TO NEW STREETS AND BUILDINGS AND THE ALTERATION OF BUILDINGS IN THE† .

Interpretation of terms.

1. Throughout these byelaws, the following words and expressions shall have the meanings hereinafter respectively assigned to them, that is to say,— **Interpretation.**

"District" means the†

"Council" means the*

"Base" applied to a wall means the under side of the course immediately above the footings:

"Topmost storey" means the uppermost storey in a building, whether constructed wholly or partly in the roof or not, and whether used or constructed or adapted for human habitation or not:

"Party wall" means:—

(*a.*) A wall forming part of a building and being used or constructed to be used in any part of the height or length of such wall for separation of adjoining buildings belonging to different owners or occupied or constructed or adapted to be occupied by different persons; or

(*b.*) A wall forming part of a building and standing, in any part of the length of such wall, to a greater extent than the projection of the footings on one side on grounds of different owners:

"External wall" means an outer wall of a building not being a party wall, even though adjoining to a wall of another building:

---

* "Mayor, aldermen, and burgesses of the borough of , acting by the Council"; *or* "Urban [*or* Rural] District Council of ," *as the case may be.*

† *Insert name of borough or urban or rural district, or, if the byelaws are to apply to part only of a rural district,* "that portion of the Rural District of which comprises the contributory places of ," *as the case may be.*

"Public building" means a building used or constructed or adapted to be used, either ordinarily or occasionally, as a church, chapel, or other place of public worship, or as a hospital, workhouse, college, school (not being merely a dwelling-house so used), theatre, public hall, public concert room, public ball-room, public lecture room, or public exhibition room, or as a public place of assembly for persons admitted thereto, by tickets or otherwise, or used or constructed or adapted to be used, either ordinarily or occasionally, for any other public purpose:

"Building of the warehouse class" means a warehouse, factory, manufactory, brewery or distillery:

"Domestic building" means a dwelling-house, or an office building or other out building appurtenant to a dwelling-house, whether attached thereto or not, or a shop, or any other building not being a public building, or of the warehouse class:

"Dwelling-house" means a building used or constructed or adapted to be used wholly or principally for human habitation:

"Width" applied to a new street, means the whole extent of space intended to be used, or laid out so as to admit of being used as a public way, exclusive of any steps or projections therein, and measured at right angles to the course or direction or intended course or direction of such street:

*"Building," when used in any byelaw with respect to waterclosets, earthclosets, privies, ashpits, or cesspools in connection with buildings, means a building erected before or after the times mentioned in section one hundred and fifty-seven of the Public Health Act, 1875:

[* Throughout the byelaws with respect to waterclosets, earthclosets, privies, ashpits, and cesspools in connection with buildings, which were made by the Council on the day of , in the year one thousand hundred and , and were confirmed by the Local

* If byelaws as to waterclosets, etc., in connection with buildings are incorporated in the present series, retain the first of these definitions. If such byelaws are already in force, the second definition will be the more suitable.

Government Board on the day of , in the year one thousand hundred and , the expression "building" shall, from and after the date of confirmation of these byelaws, mean a building erected before or after the times mentioned in section one hundred and fifty-seven of the Public Health Act, 1875.]

"Length," as applied to any timber used or intended to be used in the construction of any roof or floor, means the length of such timber in clear bearing:

"Depth," as applied to any timber used or intended to be used in the construction of any roof or floor, means the depth of such timber measured between the upper and lower surfaces of the timber when laid and fixed on edge, its greatest side being as nearly as practicable in a vertical position:

"Strength," as applied to any timber used or intended to be used in the construction of any roof or floor, means the strength represented by multiplying the depth of the timber in inches by itself, and the product by the thickness of the timber in inches.

Exempted buildings.

2. The following buildings shall be exempt from the operation of the byelaws relating to new streets and buildings:—

(*a.*) Any building in her Majesty's possession, or employed or intended to be employed for her Majesty's use or service:

(*b.*) Any county or borough lunatic asylum, and any building or part of a building belonging to the council of any county city or borough and used or intended to be used for the detention of any prisoners:

(*c.*) Any gaol, house of correction, bridewell, penitentiary, or other prison, and any building occupied or intended to be occupied by any prison officer for the use of such prison and contiguous thereto:

(*d.*) Any building (not being a dwelling-house) belonging to any person or body of persons authorised by virtue of any Act of Parliament to navigate on or use any river, canal, dock, harbour, or basin, or to demand any tolls or dues in respect of the navigation of such river or canal, or the use of such dock, harbour, or basin and used or intended to be used exclusively under the provisions of such Act of Parliament for the purposes of such river, canal, dock, harbour or basin:

(*e.*) Any building (not being a dwelling-house) erected or intended to be erected in connection with any mine, and used or intended to be used exclusively for the working of such mine:

(*f.*) Any building erected or to be erected according to plans previously approved by the Land Commissioners for England or the Board of Agriculture under the Improvement of Land Act, 1864, or other Act or Acts for the improvement of land:

(*g.*) Any building which may not be exempt by the operation of any of the preceding clauses of this byelaw, and which may be erected or may be intended to be erected in accordance with such plan and in such manner as may be approved or directed in pursuance of any statutory provision in that behalf by one of Her Majesty's Principal Secretaries of State:

(*h.*) Any building erected and used, or intended to be erected and used, exclusively for the purpose of a plant-house, orchard-house, summer-house, poultry-house, or aviary which shall be wholly detached, and at a distance of *ten feet* at the least from any other building, and which shall not be heated otherwise than by hot water, and in which the fireplaces (if any) shall be detached with no flues of any kind within such plant-house, orchard-house, summer-house, poultry-house, or aviary:

(*i.*) Any building which shall not exceed in height *thirty feet* as measured from the footings of the walls, and shall not exceed in extent *one hundred and twenty-five thousand cubic feet*, and shall not be a public building, and shall not be constructed or adapted to be used either wholly or partly for human habitation, or as a place of habitual employment for any person in any manufacture, trade, or business, and shall be distant at least *eight feet* from the nearest street, and at least *thirty feet* from the nearest building and from the boundary of any adjoining lands or premises:

(*j.*) Any building which shall exceed in height *thirty feet* as measured from the footings of the walls, and shall exceed in extent *one hundred and twenty-five thousand cubic feet*, and shall not be a public building, and shall not be constructed or adapted to be used either wholly or partly for human habitation, or as a place of habitual employment for any person in any manufacture, trade, or business, and shall be distant at least *thirty feet* from the nearest street, and at least *sixty feet* from the nearest building and from the boundary of any adjoining lands or premises:

(*k.*) Any building erected or intended to be erected for use solely as a temporary hospital for the reception and treatment of persons suffering from any dangerous infectious disorder.

To follow M. 8.

With respect to the provision, in connection with the laying out of new streets, of secondary means of access where necessary for the purpose of the removal of house refuse and other matters.

3. Every person who shall lay out a new street intended to form the principal approach or means of access to any building, shall, in connection with the laying out of such street, provide secondary means of access where necessary for the purpose of the removal of house refuse, and the contents of the receptacle of any privy or cesspool, or other matters.

Secondary means of access.

To follow M. 52.

With respect to the structure of roofs of new buildings for securing stability.

4. Every person who shall erect a new building, and shall construct the roof of such building—

Timbers of roofs of ordinary construction.

with rafters and purlins of good sound fir, or pine, laid and fixed on edge in the ordinary way;

the rafters being laid at a distance of *fifteen inches* apart, measured from the middle of one rafter to the middle of the next, or to the nearest wall;

the purlins being laid at a distance of not more than *nine feet* apart, measured from the middle of one purlin to the middle of the next, or to the ridge, or to the wall-plate; and

the roof being covered with slates of the usual kind,

shall cause the several common rafters and purlins in such roof to be, in every part, of not less depth* and thickness than are hereinafter prescribed.

Common rafters.

(1.) Subject as hereinafter provided, such person shall cause every common rafter to be of not less depth and thickness than the following, that is to say,—

Length, up to 6 ft.

(*a.*) If the length* of such rafter be not more than *six feet*, its depth shall be *three inches*, and its thickness *two inches.*

Length, 6ft. to 7 ft. 6 in.

(*b.*) If the length of such rafter be more than *six feet*, but not more than *seven feet six inches*, its depth shall be *three inches*, and its thickness *two-and-a-half inches.*

Length, 7 ft. 6 in. to 9 ft.

(*c.*) If the length of such rafter be more than *seven feet six inches*, but not more than *nine feet*, it depth shall be *four inches*, and its thickness *two-and-a-half inches.*

Purlins.

(2.) Subject as hereinafter provided, such person shall cause every purlin to be of not less depth* and thickness than the following, that is to say,—

Length, up to 6 ft. 6 in.

(*a.*) Where the length* of such purlin is not more than *six feet six inches*,—

(i.) If the distance of the purlins apart be not more than *six feet*,
the depth of the purlin shall be *four-and-a-half inches*, and
its thickness *three inches.*

(ii.) If the distance of the purlins apart be more than *six feet*, but not more than *nine feet*,
the depth of the purlin shall be *five-and-a-half inches*, and
its thickness *three inches.*

---

* The expressions "depth" and "length" are defined on p. 13.

(*b*.) Where the length of such purlin is more than *six feet six inches*, but not more than *eight feet six inches*,— Length, 6 ft. 6 in. to 8 ft. 6 in.

(i.) If the distance of the purlins apart be not more than *six feet*,
the depth of the purlin shall be *six inches*, and
its thickness *three-and-a-half inches*.

(ii.) If the distance of the purlins apart be more than *six feet*, but not more than *nine feet*,
the depth of the purlin shall be *seven inches*, and
its thickness *three-and-a-half inches*.

(*c*.) Where the length of such purlin is more than *eight feet six inches*, but not more than *ten feet six inches*,— Length, 8 ft. 6 in. to 10 ft. 6 in.

(i.) If the distance of the purlins apart be not more than *six feet*,
the depth of the purlin shall be *seven inches*, and
its thickness *four inches*.

(ii.) If the distance of the purlins apart be more than *six feet*, but not more than *nine feet*,
the depth of the purlin shall be *eight inches*, and
its thickness *four inches*.

(*d*.) Where the length of such purlin is more than *ten feet six inches*, but not more than *twelve feet six inches*,— Length, 10 ft. 6 in. to 12 ft. 6 in.

(i.) If the distance of the purlins apart be not more than *six feet*,
the depth of the purlin shall be *eight inches*, and
its thickness *five inches*.

(ii.) If the distance of the purlins apart be more than *six feet*, but not more than *nine feet*,
the depth of the purlin shall be *nine inches*, and
its thickness *five inches*.

(*e*.) Where the length of such purlin is more than *twelve feet six inches*, but not more than *fourteen feet six inches*,— Length, 12 ft. 6 in. to 14 ft. 6 in.

(i.) If the distance of the purlins apart be not more than *six feet*,
the depth of the purlin shall be *nine inches*, and
its thickness *five inches*.

(ii.) If the distance of the purlins apart be more than *six feet*, but not more than *nine feet*,
the depth of the purlin shall be *ten inches*, and its thickness *five-and-a-half inches*.

Length, 14 ft. 6 in. to 16 ft. 6 in.

(*f*.) Where the length of such purlin is more than *fourteen feet six inches*, but not more than *sixteen feet six inches*,—

(i.) If the distance of the purlins apart be not more than *six feet*,
the depth of the purlin shall be *ten inches*, and its thickness *five-and-a-half inches*.

(ii.) If the distance of the purlins apart be more than *six feet*, but not more than *nine feet*,
the depth of the purlin shall be *eleven inches*, and its thickness *six inches*.

Length, over 16 ft. 6 in.

(*g*.) Where the length of such purlin is more than *sixteen feet six inches*, such purlin shall be of such greater strength as shall be sufficient to secure proper stability, having regard to the distance of the purlins apart.

Provided that,—

Roofs (common rafters and purlins). Proviso for timbers of the same strength;

(1.) the foregoing requirements of this byelaw as regards the depth and thickness of rafters and purlins shall be deemed to be complied with, if the person erecting the new building shall cause the several rafters and purlins to be of at least the same strength* as is required by the byelaw:

and for timbers of a less strength.

(2.) if the rafters be laid at a less distance apart than that specified in this byelaw, they may be of proportionately less strength* than is required by the byelaw.

Timbers of certain roofs not within the preceding byelaw.

5. Every person who shall erect a new building, and

who shall construct the roof of such building with rafters and purlins laid at a greater distance apart than that specified in the foregoing byelaw, but otherwise in the manner specified in such byelaw, or

who shall cause such roof to be covered with tiles or lead, shall cause such rafters and purlins to be of proportionately greater strength* than is required by such byelaw.

---

* "Strength" is defined on p. 13.

6. Every person who shall erect a new building, and shall cause the roof of such building (not being a boarded roof) to be covered with slates, shall cause the slates to be secured to sawn battens not less than *two inches* in depth and *three-quarters of an inch* in thickness. **Roof battens.**

7. Every person who shall erect a new building, and shall cause the roof of such building to be covered with slates or tiles, shall cause such slates or tiles to be properly laid so as to break joint, and so that each course of slates or tiles shall overlap the course next but one below it to the extent of not less than *three inches*. **Laying and fixing of slates or tiles.**

If he shall cause such roof to be covered with slates, he shall cause every slate to be secured by not less than two strong copper, galvanised, or other suitable nails, at least *two inches* in length.

To follow M. 52.

With respect to the structure of floors, hearths, and staircases, and the height of rooms intended to be used for human habitation.

FLOORS.

8. Every person who shall erect a new building, and shall construct any floor in such building— **Timbers of floors of ordinary construction.**

with joists, or joists and beams or girders of good sound fir or pine, laid on edge in the ordinary way,

the joists being laid at a distance of *fifteen inches* apart, measured from the middle of one joist to the middle of the next, or to the nearest wall,

the beams or girders being laid at a distance of *ten feet* apart, measured from the middle of one beam or girder to the middle of the next, or to the nearest wall, and

the joists being covered with boards,

shall cause the several common joists in such floor, and the several beams or girders supporting the same, and not supporting any wall, pier, or other such load, to have a sufficient bearing at each end, and to be, in every part, of not less depth and thickness than are hereinafter prescribed.

(1.) Subject as hereinafter provided, such person shall, if such building be a domestic building, cause every common **Common joists (domestic buildings).**

joist to be of not less depth and thickness than the following, that is to say,—

Length, up to 4 ft.

(*a.*) If the length* of such joist be not more than *four feet*,
its depth shall be *four inches*, and
its thickness *two inches*.

Length, 4 ft. to 6 ft.

(*b.*) If the length of such joist be more than *four feet*, but not more than *six feet*,
its depth shall be *four and a half inches*, and
its thickness *two inches*.

Length, 6 ft. to 8 ft.

(*c.*) If the length of such joist be more than *six feet*, but not more than *eight feet*,
its depth shall be *four and a half inches*, and
its thickness *two and a half inches*.

Length, 8 ft. to 10 ft.

(*d.*) If the length of such joist be more than *eight feet*, but not more than *ten feet*,
its depth shall be *five inches*, and
its thickness *two and a half inches*.

Length, 10 ft. to 12 ft.

(*e.*) If the length of such joist be more than *ten feet*, but not more than *twelve feet*,
its depth shall be *six inches*, and
its thickness *two and a half inches*.

Length, 12 ft. to 14 ft.

(*f.*) If the length of such joist be more than *twelve feet*, but not more than *fourteen feet*,
its depth shall be *seven inches*, and
its thickness *two and a half inches*.

Length, 14 ft. to 15 feet.

(*g.*) If the length of such joist be more than *fourteen feet*, but not more than *fifteen feet*,
its depth shall be *seven inches*, and
its thickness *three inches*.

Length, 15 ft. to 17 ft.

(*h.*) If the length of such joist be more than *fifteen feet*, but not more than *seventeen feet*,
its depth shall be *seven and a half inches*, and
its thickness *three inches*.

Length, 17 ft. to 19 ft.

(*i.*) If the length of such joist be more than *seventeen feet*, but not more than *nineteen feet*,
its depth shall be *eight inches*, and
its thickness *three inches*.

Length, 19 ft. to 21 ft.

(*j.*) If the length of such joist be more than *nineteen feet*, but not more than *twenty-one feet*,
its depth shall be *nine inches*, and
its thickness *three inches*.

---

* "Length" is defined on p. 13.

(*k.*) If the length of such joist be more than *twenty-one feet*, but not more than *twenty-three feet*, Length, 21 ft. to 23 ft.
its depth shall be *ten inches*, and
its thickness *three inches*.

(*l.*) If the length of such joist be more than *twenty-three feet*, such joist shall be of such greater strength as shall be sufficient to secure proper stability. Length, over 23 ft.

(2.) Subject as hereinafter provided, such person shall if such building be a building of the warehouse class, cause every common joist to be of not less depth and thickness than the following, that is to say,— Common joists (warehouse buildings).

(*a.*) If the length* of such joist be not more than *four feet*, Length, up to 4 ft.
its depth shall be *four and a half inches*, and
its thickness *three inches*.

(*b.*) If the length of such joist be more than *four feet*, but not more than *six feet*, Length, 4 ft. to 6 ft.
its depth shall be *six inches*, and
its thickness *three inches*.

(*c.*) If the length of such joist be more than *six feet*, but not more than *nine feet*, Length, 6 ft. to 9 ft.
its depth shall be *eight inches*, and
its thickness *three inches*.

(*d.*) If the length of such joist be more than *nine feet*, but not more than *twelve feet*, Length, 9 ft. to 12 ft.
its depth shall be *ten inches*, and
its thickness *three inches*.

(*e.*) If the length of such joist be more than *twelve feet*, and not more than *fifteen feet*, Length, 12 ft. to 15 ft.
its depth shall be *eleven inches*, and
its thickness *three inches*.

(*f.*) If the length of such joist be more than *fifteen feet*, but not more than *eighteen feet*, Length, 15 ft. to 18 ft.
its depth shall be *thirteen inches*, and
its thickness *three and a half inches*.

(*g.*) If the length of such joist be more than *eighteen feet*, but not more than *twenty feet*, Length, 18 ft. to 20 ft.
its depth shall be *thirteen inches*, and
its thickness *four inches*.

(*h.*) If the length of such joist be more than *twenty feet*, such joist shall be of such greater strength as shall be sufficient to secure proper stability. Length, over 20 ft.

---

* "Length" is defined on p. 13.

Trimmer and trimming joists (domestic buildings).

(3.) Subject as hereinafter provided, such person shall, if such building be a domestic building, cause every trimmer joist receiving or carrying not more than six common joists, and every trimming joist receiving or carrying any such trimmer joist at a distance not greater than *three feet* from its bearing on the wall, to be of a depth not less than the depth, and of a thickness at least *one inch* greater than the thickness hereinbefore required in the case of a domestic building for a common joist of the same length.

He shall not cause the extra thickness to be added in a separate scantling, but shall cause such trimmer or trimming joist to be solid throughout.

He shall not cause any trimmer joist for an opening in connection with a flue or fireplace, to receive or carry more than six common joists.

He shall cause every trimmer joist receiving or carrying more than six common joists, and every trimming joist receiving or carrying such trimmer, to be of such greater strength as shall be sufficient to secure proper stability.

Trimmer and trimming joists (warehouse buildings).

(4.) Subject as hereinafter provided, such person shall, if such building be a building of the warehouse class, cause every trimmer joist receiving or carrying not more than six common joists, to be of a depth not less than the depth, and of a thickness at least *one quarter of an inch* greater for each common joist which it receives or carries, than the thickness hereinbefore required, in the case of a building of the warehouse class, for a common joist of the same length.

He shall cause every trimming joist receiving or carrying any such trimmer joist, at a distance not greater than *three feet* from its bearing on the wall, to be of a depth not less than the depth, and of a thickness at least *one inch and-a-half* greater than the thickness hereinbefore required, in the case of a building of the warehouse class, for a common joist of the same length.

He shall not cause the extra thickness to be added in a separate scantling, but shall cause such trimmer or trimming joist to be solid throughout.

(5.) Subject as hereinafter provided, such person shall, if such building be a domestic building, cause every beam or girder supporting such floor, and not supporting any wall, pier, or other such load, to be in every part of not less depth and thickness than the following, that is to say,— **Beams, etc. (domestic buildings).**

(*a.*) If the length* of such beam or girder be not more than *ten feet*, **Length, up to 10 ft.**
its depth shall be *nine inches*, and
its thickness *six inches*.

(*b.*) If the length of such beam or girder be more than *ten feet*, but not more than *twelve feet*, **Length, 10 ft. to 12 ft.**
its depth shall be *ten inches*, and
its thickness *seven inches*.

(*c.*) If the length of such beam or girder be more than *twelve feet*, but not more than *fourteen feet*, **Length, 12 ft. to 14 ft.**
its depth shall be *eleven inches*, and
its thickness *eight inches*.

(*d.*) If the length of such beam or girder be more than *fourteen feet*, but not more than *sixteen feet*, **Length, 14 ft. to 16 ft.**
its depth shall be *twelve inches*, and
its thickness *nine inches*.

(*e.*) If the length of such beam or girder be more than *sixteen feet*, such beam or girder shall be of such greater strength as shall be sufficient to secure proper stability. **Length, over 16 ft.**

(6.) Subject as hereinafter provided, such person shall, if such building be a building of the warehouse class, cause every beam or girder supporting such floor, and not supporting any wall, pier, or other such load, to be in every part of not less depth and thickness than the following, that is to say,— **Beams, etc. (warehouse buildings).**

(*a.*) If the length* of such beam or girder be not more than *ten feet*, **Length, up to 10 ft.**
its depth shall be *twelve inches*, and
its thickness *ten inches*.

(*b.*) If the length of such beam or girder be more than *ten feet*, but not more than *twelve feet*, **Length, 10 ft. to 12 ft.**
its depth shall be *thirteen inches*, and
its thickness *eleven inches*.

* "Length" is defined on p. 13.

Length, 12 ft. to 14 ft.

(c.) If the length of such beam or girder be more than *twelve feet*, but not more than *fourteen feet*, its depth shall be *fourteen inches*, and its thickness *twelve inches*.

Length, 14 ft. to 16 ft.

(d.) If the length of such beam or girder be more than *fourteen feet*, but not more than *sixteen feet*, its depth shall be *fifteen inches*, and its thickness *thirteen inches*.

Length, over 16 feet.

(e.) If the length of such beam or girder be more than *sixteen feet*, such beam or girder shall be of such greater strength as shall be sufficient to secure proper stability.

Provided that,—

Floors (joists and beams, etc.). Proviso for timbers of the same strength,

(1.) the foregoing requirements of this byelaw as regards the depth and thickness of joists and beams or girders, shall be deemed to be complied with if the person erecting the new building shall cause the several joists and beams or girders to be of at least the same strength* as is required by the byelaw; and the thickness of the joist, or of the beam or girder, be in no case less than two-thirds of the thickness hereinbefore specified:

and for timbers of a less strength.

(2.) if the joists and beams or girders be laid at a less distance apart than that specified in this byelaw, they may be of proportionately less strength* than is required by the byelaw; but the thickness of the several joists and beams or girders shall in no case be less than two-thirds of the thickness hereinbefore specified.

Timbers of certain floors not within the preceding byelaw.

9.—(1.) Every person who shall erect a new building, and shall construct any floor in such building,—

with joists, or joists and beams or girders laid at a greater distance apart than that specified in the foregoing byelaw, but

otherwise in the manner specified in such byelaw,

shall cause such joists, or joists and beams or girders to be of proportionately greater strength* than is required by such byelaw; and

(2.) every person who shall erect a new building, and shall construct any floor in such building—

as a framed floor, or

* "Strength" is defined on p. 13.

as a floor formed with beams at short distances apart, and covered with battens, deals, or planks, without joists, or

with joists covered with boards, where the joists, or joists and beams or girders are of any kind of wood not being good sound fir or pine;

shall cause the several timbers of such floor to be of such depth and thickness as to secure proper stability.

10. Every person who shall erect a new public building, or a new building of the warehouse class, shall cause every floor of such building, not being a floor to which any of the foregoing byelaws apply, to be properly constructed of sound and suitable materials and of adequate strength.

Floors (public and warehouse buildings).

He shall, in the case of a public building, cause the floor of every lobby, passage, corridor, or landing therein which is not intended solely as a means of access to any private apartment, to be constructed of incombustible materials, and carried by supports of incombustible material.

11.—(1.) Every person who shall erect a new building, and shall construct any floor in such building of joists covered with boards, shall, where the length of the joists exceeds *seven feet* and does not exceed *twelve feet*, cause at least *one row* of square bridging or herring-bone strutting to be constructed between the joists:

Bridging or strutting.

Where the length of the joists exceeds *twelve feet* and does not exceed *eighteen feet*, he shall cause at least *two rows* of square bridging or herring-bone strutting to be so constructed; and

Where the length of the joists exceeds *eighteen feet*, he shall, for every *six feet* or part of six feet over eighteen feet, cause at least one additional row of square bridging or herring-bone strutting to be so constructed.

(2.) He shall cause any such bridging to be formed of good sound and suitable timber, and to be of a depth equal to the depth of the joists, and of a thickness not less than *one and a half inch*.

(3.) He shall cause any such strutting to be formed of good sound and suitable timber, of a depth not less than *two inches*, and of a thickness not less than *one and a quarter inch*.

Floor boards (domestic buildings).

12. Every person who shall erect a new domestic building, and shall in such building construct any boarded floor, shall cause such floor to be laid with boards not less than *seven-eighths of an inch* in actual thickness: provided that in the case of a room which is intended to be used as a sleeping-room only, the floor may be laid with boards not less than *three-quarters of an inch* in actual thickness.

To follow M. 52.

HEARTHS.

Hearths.

13. Every person who shall construct a hearth in a building shall cause such hearth to be of stone, slate, tiles, or other incombustible substance, and to be laid level with the upper surface of the floor adjacent to such hearth.

He shall cause such hearth to be at least *six inches* longer on each side than the width of the chimney opening in front of which it is placed, and to extend outwards from the chimney breast to a distance of at least *eighteen inches.*

He shall cause such hearth to be bedded wholly on brick, stone, concrete, or other incombustible substance, extending to a depth of not less than *seven inches* from the upper surface of the hearth, and to be properly supported upon bearers of stone or iron, or upon brick trimmers or other incombustible materials: provided that if such hearth be in the lowest storey of the building, he may cause such hearth to be bedded on the solid ground.

To follow M. 52.

STAIRCASES.

Staircases (domestic buildings).

14. Every person who shall erect a new domestic building, and shall construct any staircase therein, shall comply with the following requirements, that is to say,—

(1.) He shall cause the woodwork of every flight of stairs in such staircase to be of not less than the following thicknesses, namely,—

(*a.*) the strings shall be not less than *one inch and a quarter* in thickness:

(*b.*) the treads shall be not less than *one inch* in thickness:

(*c.*) the risers shall be not less than *three-quarters of an inch* in thickness.

(2.) He shall cause the treads to be not less than *eight inches* in width, measured horizontally, from face of riser to face of riser, and the risers to be not more than *nine inches* in height, measured vertically from top of tread to top of tread.

(3.) He shall cause such staircase to be provided with a sufficient handrail properly and securely fixed.

15. Every person who shall erect a new public building, or a new building of the warehouse class, and shall construct any staircase therein, shall cause every flight of stairs in such staircase to be properly constructed of sound and suitable materials, and to be securely fixed, and of adequate strength. **Staircases (public and warehouse buildings).**

He shall, in the case of a public building, cause every flight of stairs in such staircase which is not intended solely as a means of access to any private apartment, to be constructed of incombustible materials and carried by supports of incombustible material, and to be furnished on each side with a sufficient handrail properly and securely fixed.

He shall, in the case of a public building, cause every flight of stairs in such staircase which is intended solely as a means of access to any private apartments, to be provided with a sufficient handrail properly and securely fixed.

To follow M. 52.

Height of Rooms.

16. Every person who shall erect a new building shall construct every room in such building which shall be intended to be used for human habitation, in accordance with such of the following regulations as may be applicable to the circumstances of the case, that is to say,— **Height of rooms.**

(1.) Every such room which is an attic, or a room wholly or partly in the roof of such building, shall, over at least *two-thirds* of the area of the floor, be not less than *nine feet* in height, and shall not in any part be less than *five feet* in height:

(2.) Every such room which is not an attic, or a room wholly or partly in the roof of such building, shall not in any part be less than *eight feet six inches* in height.

To follow M. 59.

With respect to the paving of yards and open spaces in connection with dwelling-houses.

17. The owner of every dwelling-house in connection with which there is any yard or open space shall, where it is necessary for the prevention or remedy of insanitary conditions that all or part of such yard or open space shall be paved, forthwith cause the same to be properly paved with a hard, durable, and impervious pavement of flagging or paving bricks evenly and closely laid upon a sufficient bed of good concrete, mortar, or other suitable material, and properly jointed, or with good cement concrete, or with good asphalt on a proper foundation, and so sloped to a properly constructed channel as effectually to carry off all rain or waste water therefrom.

18. Every person who shall erect a new dwelling-house shall cause not less than *one hundred and fifty square feet* of any open space, provided in connection therewith, to be paved with a hard, durable, and impervious pavement of flagging or paving bricks, evenly and closely laid upon a sufficient bed of good concrete, mortar, or other suitable material, and properly jointed, or with good cement concrete, or with good asphalt on a proper foundation, and so sloped to a properly constructed channel as effectually to carry away all rain and waste water that may fall thereon.

He shall cause such paving to be so arranged that it shall adjoin the external wall in the rear or at the side of the dwelling-house, that, wherever practicable, it shall extend throughout to a distance of *ten feet* from the said wall, and that, subject to this last-mentioned requirement, it shall extend as nearly as conveniently may be to the full width of the open space.

For the purposes of this byelaw the expression "width" means, in the case of paving in the rear, a measurement taken parallel to the rear external wall of the dwelling-house, and, in the case of paving at the side, a measurement taken at right angles to the side external wall on which such paving may abut:

Provided always, that, in the case of any dwelling-house, the height of which is less than *fifteen feet* as measured from the level of the open space to the level of half the vertical height of the roof or to the top of the parapet, whichever may be the higher, any part of an open space provided in pursuance of any byelaw in that behalf which is occupied by any water-closet, earthcloset, or privy, and ashpit may be reckoned as if it were paved, if the remainder of such open space is paved in accordance with this byelaw.

To follow M. 89.

With respect to the keeping waterclosets supplied with sufficient water for flushing.

19. The occupier of any premises in or for which a watercloset is for the time being provided, shall cause such watercloset to be at all times properly supplied with a sufficient quantity of water for the proper flushing thereof. Flushing of waterclosets.

Where, however, any watercloset is provided for the use of persons occupying two or more separately occupied premises, and there is a person having the charge and control of such watercloset, the foregoing requirement shall apply to such person.

The person in occupation of or having the charge, management, or control of the premises, or if there is no such person, then any person in occupation of or having the charge, management, or control of any part of the premises, and in the case of any premises the whole of which is let to lodgers, the person receiving the rent payable by the lodgers, either on his own account or as the agent of another person, shall for the purpose of this byelaw be deemed to be the occupier.

This byelaw shall apply to any building in or for which a watercloset is for the time being provided, whether such building is a building erected before or after the times mentioned in section 157 of the Public Health Act, 1875.

To follow M. 91.

As to the deposit of plans by persons intending to lay out streets.

20. Every person who shall intend to lay out a street intended to form the principal approach or means of access to any building, shall show on every plan of such street which, in pursuance of any byelaw in that behalf, he may be required to deliver or send to the clerk or surveyor of the Council, the secondary means of access proposed to be provided in connection with the laying out of such street, where necessary for the removal of house refuse and other matters. Deposit of plans.

To follow M. 97.

For preventing buildings which have been erected in accordance with byelaws made under the Public Health Acts from being altered in such a way that if at first so constructed they would have contravened the byelaws.

21. A person shall not alter any building which has been erected in accordance with byelaws made under the Public Alteration of buildings.

Health Acts in such a way that, if at first constructed as altered, such building would have contravened such byelaws.

Notice of intention to alter building. Deposit of plans and sections.

22. Every person who shall intend to alter a building which has been erected in accordance with byelaws made under the Public Health Acts shall give to the Council notice in writing of such intention, which shall be delivered or sent to their clerk at his or their office, or to their surveyor at his or their office, and shall at the same time deliver or send, or cause to be delivered or sent to their clerk at his or their office, or to their surveyor at his or their office, complete plans and sections of such intended alteration, which shall be drawn in duplicate, in ink on tracing cloth, or otherwise in a suitable manner and on suitable material, to a scale of not less than *one inch* to every *eight feet*, and shall show the position, form, and dimensions of the several parts of such building, in or in connection with which such alteration is intended to be made, and in such plan and sections he shall cause such building to be so described as to show whether the building, as proposed to be altered, is intended to be used as a dwelling-house or otherwise.

Such person shall at the same time deliver or send, or cause to be delivered or sent to the clerk to the Council at his or their office, or to their surveyor at his or their office, a description in writing of the materials of or with which it is intended that such alteration shall be constructed.

Such person shall, in every case where necessary for the purpose of such alteration, at the same time deliver or send, or cause to be delivered or sent to the clerk to the Council at his or their office, or to their surveyor at his or their office, a block plan of such intended alteration which shall be drawn in duplicate, in ink on tracing cloth, or otherwise in a suitable manner and on suitable material, to a scale of not less than *one inch* to every *forty-four feet;* and so far as may be necessary for the purposes of such alteration, he shall show on such block plan the position of the buildings and appurtenances of the properties immediately adjoining, the width and level of the street in front, and of the street, if any, at the rear of such building, the level of the lowest floor of such building, and of any yard or ground belonging thereto, and also the lines or intended lines of drainage of such building, and the size, depth, and inclination or intended size, depth, and inclination of each drain, and the details of the arrangement adopted or proposed to be adopted for the ventilation of the drains.

23. Every person who shall intend to alter a building which has been erected in accordance with byelaws made under the Public Health Acts, shall before beginning to execute any work in connection with such intended alteration, deliver or send, or cause to be delivered or sent to the surveyor of the Council at his or their office notice in writing, in which shall be specified the date on which such person will begin to execute such work.

Notice before commencing the work, etc.

Such person shall also, before proceeding to cover up any drain, or any foundation, deliver or send, or cause to be delivered or sent to the surveyor of the Council at his or their office notice in writing, in which shall be specified the date on which such person will proceed to cover up such drain or foundation.

24. In every case:—

Notice to amend work;

Where a person who shall alter a building which has been erected in accordance with byelaws made under the Public Health Acts, shall, at any reasonable time during the progress or after the completion of the work of alteration of such building, receive from the surveyor of the Council notice in writing specifying any matters in respect of which such building as altered by such work, would, if at first so constructed, have contravened such byelaws, and requiring such person within a reasonable time, which shall be specified in such notice, to cause anything done contrary to such byelaws to be amended, or to do anything which by such byelaws would have been required to be done and which has been omitted to be done:—

Such person shall, within the time specified in such notice, comply with the several requirements thereof so far as such requirements relate to matters in respect of which such building, as so altered, would, if at first so constructed, have contravened such byelaws.

and of completion of requirements.

Such person, within a reasonable time after the completion of any work which may have been executed in accordance with any such requirement, shall deliver or send, or cause to be delivered or sent, to the surveyor of the Council at his or their office notice in writing of the completion of such work, and shall, at all reasonable times within a period of *seven days* after such notice shall have been so delivered or sent, afford such surveyor free access to such work for the purpose of inspection.

Inspection during progress of work.

25. Every person who shall alter a building which has been erected in accordance with byelaws made under the Public

Health Acts, shall, at all reasonable times, during the work of alteration, afford the surveyor of the Council free access to such building for the purpose of inspecting such work.

Inspection on completion of work.

26. Every person who shall alter a building which has been erected in accordance with byelaws made under the Public Health Acts shall, within a reasonable time after the completion of the work of alteration, deliver or send, or cause to be delivered or sent, to the surveyor of the Council, at his or their office, notice in writing of the completion of such work, and shall, at all reasonable times, within a period of *seven days* after such notice shall have been so delivered or sent, afford such surveyor free access to such building for the purpose of inspecting such work.

Penalties.

27. Every person who shall offend against any of the foregoing byelaws shall be liable for every such offence to a penalty of *five pounds*, and in the case of a continuing offence to a further penalty of *forty shillings* for each day after written notice of the offence from the Council:

Provided, nevertheless, that the justices or court before whom any complaint may be made or any proceedings may be taken in respect of any such offence may, if they think fit, adjudge the payment as a penalty of any sum less than the full amount of the penalty imposed by this byelaw.

As to the power of the Council to remove, alter, or pull down any work begun or done in contravention of certain byelaws.

Power to pull down work.

28. If any work to which any of the foregoing byelaws numbered *three* to *twenty** both inclusive, may apply be begun or done in contravention of any such byelaw, the person by whom such work shall be so begun or done, by a notice in writing, which shall be signed by the clerk to the Council, and shall be duly served upon or delivered to such person, shall be required on or before such day as shall be specified in such notice by a statement in writing under his hand or under the hand of an agent duly authorised in that behalf, and addressed to and duly served upon the Council, to show sufficient cause

* Verify these numbers. See the memorandum prefixed to this series (p. 10).

why such work shall not be removed, altered, or pulled down; or shall be required on such day and at such time and place as shall be specified in such notice to attend personally or by an agent duly authorised in that behalf before the Council and show sufficient cause why such work shall not be removed, altered, or pulled down.

If such person shall fail to show sufficient cause why such work shall not be removed, altered, or pulled down, the Council shall be empowered, subject to any statutory provision in that behalf, to remove, alter, or pull down such work.

PART II.

TENT AND VAN DWELLINGS

AND

HOUSING OF HOP-PICKERS, FRUIT-PICKERS, AND OTHERS.

TENT AND VAN DWELLINGS.

MEMORANDUM

of the Local Government Board with respect to tents, vans, etc.

Section 9 of the Housing of the Working Classes Act, 1885 (48 & 49 Vict. c. 72), provides that,—

* * * * *

"(2.) A sanitary authority may make byelaws for promoting cleanliness in, and the habitable condition of tents, vans, sheds, and similar structures used for human habitation, and for preventing the spread of infectious disease by the persons inhabiting the same, and generally for the prevention of nuisances in connection with the same.

* * * * *

"Nothing in this section shall apply to any tent, van, shed, or structure, erected or used by any portion of Her Majesty's military or naval forces."

Similar provisions are contained in sub-sections (2) and (4) of section 95 of the Public Health (London) Act, 1891 (54 & 55 Vict. c. 76).

The Local Authorities authorised by the above-mentioned enactments to make byelaws are, elsewhere than in London, the Council of any Borough or Urban or Rural District, and in London, any Sanitary Authority as defined by section 99 of the Public Health (London) Act, 1891.

Byelaws made under either of the Acts referred to require confirmation by the Local Government Board (48 & 49 Vict. c. 72, s. 10 (1); 54 & 55 Vict. c. 76, s. 114).

With a view to the better enforcement of the provisions of the former Act, and of any byelaws made by a Local Authority thereunder, sub-section 9 (3) enacts that,—

"Where any person duly authorised by a sanitary authority or by a justice of the peace has reasonable cause to suppose either that there is any contravention of the provisions of this Act, or any byelaw made under this Act, in any tent, van, shed, or similar structure, used for human habitation, or that there is in any such tent, van, shed, or structure any person suffering from a dangerous infectious disorder, he may, on producing (if demanded) either a copy of his authorisation purporting to be certified by the clerk or a member of the sanitary authority or some other sufficient evidence of his being authorised as aforesaid, enter by day such tent, van, shed, or structure, and examine the same and every part thereof in order to ascertain whether in such tent, van, shed, or structure there is any contravention of any such byelaw or a person suffering from a dangerous infectious disorder."

Corresponding provisions applicable to London are contained in section 95 (3) of the Public Health (London) Act, 1891.

Local Government Board,
May, 1899.

MODEL BYELAWS OF THE LOCAL GOVERNMENT BOARD AS TO TENTS, VANS, ETC.

BYELAWS

MADE BY THE* WITH RESPECT TO TENTS, VANS, SHEDS, AND SIMILAR STRUCTURES.

Interpretation of terms.

1. Throughout these byelaws the expression "the Council" means the * ; the expression "the District" means the† ; the expression "infectious disease" means small-pox, cholera, diphtheria, membranous croup, erysipelas, the disease known as scarlatina or scarlet fever, measles, and the fevers known by any of the following names: typhus, typhoid, enteric, relapsing, continued, or puerperal; the expression "the Medical Officer of Health" means the Medical Officer of Health for the District, or any legally qualified medical practitioner lawfully authorised to act on behalf of such officer; and the expression "the occupier" when used in relation to any tent, van, shed, or similar structure, means the person who for the time being has the charge, management, or control of such tent, van, shed or structure. Interpretation.

Definition of "occupier."—In some cases the definition of "occupier" prescribed by this byelaw will indicate the owner or lessee of the land on which the tent, van, shed, or structure is erected or placed, as the person who is liable to the penalties imposed by the byelaws; but in the case of gipsies and other persons using their own tents or vans, the model series as printed imposes no duty on the owner or lessee of the land. It would, however, appear to be reasonable under certain circumstances that this person should be brought within the scope of the byelaws; and it is believed that certain Local Authorities have, with the approval of the Local Government Board, made byelaws imposing on him duties in connection with the provision of a water supply, an ashpit, and sufficient privy accommodation for the use of the occupants of any tent, van, shed, or similar structure used for human habitation that may be erected or brought upon his land with his knowledge, licence or consent.

---

* "Mayor, aldermen, and burgesses of the borough of , acting by the Council"; *or*, "Urban [*or* Rural] District Council of ," *as the case may be.*

† "Borough of " *or* "Urban [*or* Rural] District of ," *as the case may be.*

For promoting cleanliness in and the habitable condition of tents, vans, sheds, and similar structures used for human habitation.

Cleansing of vans.

2. The occupier of a van used for human habitation shall cause the internal surface and the floor thereof to be thoroughly cleansed from time to time as often as may be requisite for keeping the same in a cleanly condition.

Ventilation of vans, sheds, etc.

3. The occupier of a van, shed or similar structure used for human habitation, shall for the purpose of securing the habitable condition thereof, provide for such van, shed, or structure, adequate means of permanent ventilation.

Structures to be weather-proof.

4. The occupier of a tent, van, shed or similar structure used for human habitation, shall cause the same to be maintained so that it may be reasonably weather-proof at all times when so used.

Floor or ground covering for tents, sheds, etc.

5. The occupier of a tent, shed or similar structure used for human habitation, shall cause the same to be at all times provided with a suitable dry flooring, or other dry covering for the ground.

Water supply and storage.

6. The occupier of a tent, van, shed or similar structure used for human habitation shall provide therefor a sufficient receptacle or receptacles for the storage of water, with proper coverings, so placed as to be easily accessible, and shall cause the same to be maintained at all times in good order, and shall provide a sufficient supply of wholesome water for the use of the inmates of such tent, van, shed or structure, and shall also cause every part of the interior of any such receptacle to be kept thoroughly clean.

For preventing the spread of infectious disease by the persons inhabiting tents, vans, sheds, or similar structures used for human habitation.

Infectious disease.—Notification.

7. The occupier of a tent, van, shed or similar structure used for human habitation who shall have been informed, or shall have ascertained, that any inmate thereof is ill of an infectious disease, shall thereupon immediately give notice to the Medical Officer of Health.

Provided that this byelaw shall not apply in respect of any infectious disease of which any such notice is required to be given by any statutory provision in force in the District.*

Directions of Medical Officer of Health to be complied with.

8. The occupier of a tent, van, shed or similar structure used for human habitation who shall have been informed or shall have ascertained that any inmate thereof is ill of an infectious disease, shall adopt all reasonable precautions that may be ordered by the Medical Officer of Health for preventing the spread of such disease.

Isolation of patient.

He shall not, at any time while such inmate is suffering from such infectious disease, cause or allow any other person, except a person in attendance on such inmate, to occupy such tent, van, shed or similar structure.

Movement of infected tent or van.

9. The occupier of a tent or van used for human habitation, in which any person may within the preceding six weeks have been suffering from an infectious disease, and which has not since been properly disinfected, or in which any person is at the time suffering from an infectious disease, shall comply with the following regulations:—

(1.) He shall, before causing or allowing such tent or van to be removed from the site on which it may be, give to the Medical Officer of Health twenty-four hours' notice of the intention to remove the same, and of the place to which the same is proposed to be removed.

(2.) He shall not cause or allow such tent or van to be brought into any market, fair, race-ground or place which may for the time being be devoted to purposes of public amusement, recreation or resort, or to be removed to any site where, in the opinion of the Medical Officer of Health, there would be danger of spreading infection.

(3.) He shall, where the Medical Officer of Health may for the purpose of preventing the spread of infection, order the removal of such tent or van from any site, remove the same, in compliance with the order of the Medical Officer of Health, to another site within the district to which it may lawfully be removed.

---

* See the Infectious Disease (Notification) Act, 1889, and the provisions of s. 55 of the Public Health (London) Act, 1891.

(4.) He shall, when removing such tent or van, comply with such reasonable conditions as the Medical Officer of Health may impose, for the purpose of preventing the spread of infection.

(5.) He shall not remove such tent or van out of the district until the same has been properly disinfected.

Removal of patient to hospital.

10. In every case where, in pursuance of any statutory provision in that behalf, an order of a justice has been obtained for the removal from a tent, van, shed or similar structure used for human habitation to a hospital, or other place for the reception of the sick, of a person who is suffering from any dangerous infectious disorder, the occupier of such tent, van, shed or structure shall, on being informed of such order, forthwith take all such steps as may be requisite to secure the safe and prompt removal of such person in compliance with such order, and shall, in and about such removal, adopt all such precautions as, in accordance with any instructions which he may receive from the Medical Officer of Health, may be most suitable for the circumstances of the case.

Cleansing and disinfection.

11. The occupier of a tent, van, shed or similar structure used for human habitation shall, immediately after a person suffering from an infectious disease has been removed therefrom, or has died therein, or has recovered from such disease whilst being therein, give notice of such removal, death, or recovery to the Medical Officer of Health, and shall, as soon as conveniently may be, cause every part of such tent, van, shed or structure to be thoroughly cleansed and disinfected, and shall also cause all bedding, clothing, or other articles therein which may be liable to retain infection to be in like manner cleansed and disinfected unless the Council shall have ordered the same to be destroyed, or unless the Council or the Medical Officer of Health shall, in pursuance of any statutory provision in that behalf, have required the owner of the same to cause the same to be delivered to an officer of the Council for removal for the purpose of disinfection.

He shall comply with all proper instructions of the Medical Officer of Health as to cleansing and disinfection.

When the tent, van, shed, or similar structure, and every such article as aforesaid shall have been thoroughly cleansed and disinfected in accordance with such instructions, he shall give notice thereof to the Medical Officer of Health.

12. The occupier of a tent, van, shed, or similar structure used for human habitation, in which any person has within six weeks previously been suffering from an infectious disease, shall not without having such tent, van, shed, or similar structure, and all articles therein liable to retain infection, disinfected to the satisfaction of a registered medical practitioner as testified by a certificate signed by him, cause or suffer any person newly to occupy or become an inmate of such tent, van, shed, or similar structure.

Re-occupation of tent, van, shed, etc.

Generally for preventing nuisances in connection with tents, vans, sheds, and similar structures used for human habitation.

13. The occupier of a tent, van, shed or similar structure used for human habitation, shall provide a sufficient receptacle for refuse for the same.

Provision of receptacle for refuse.

14. An occupier of a tent, van, shed or similar structure used for human habitation shall not cause or suffer any solid or liquid filth to be retained therein.

Retention, removal, and deposit of filth.

He shall not deposit or cause any solid or liquid filth to be deposited within *thirty feet* from such tent, van, shed or structure, or in any other place so as to cause a nuisance.

He shall cause every vessel, utensil, or other receptacle provided or used for the purpose of containing or removing any solid or liquid filth to be sufficiently cleansed immediately after the same shall have been used for such purpose.

15. The occupier of a tent, van, shed or similar structure used for human habitation shall not keep any animal or deposit any filth or the dung of any animal within the distance of *forty feet* from any well, spring, or stream, or other water used or likely to be used by man for drinking or domestic purposes, or for manufacturing drinks for the use of man, or any water used or likely to be used in any dairy, or otherwise in such a position or in such a manner as to render any such water liable to pollution.

Protection of water.

Penalties.

16. Every person who shall offend against any of the foregoing byelaws shall be liable for every such offence to a penalty

Penalties.

of *five pounds*, and in the case of a continuing offence to a further penalty of *forty shillings* for each day after written notice of the offence from the Council.

Provided, nevertheless, that the justices or court before whom any complaint may be made, or any proceedings may be taken in respect of any such offence, may, if they think fit, adjudge the payment as a penalty of any sum less than the full amount of the penalty imposed by this byelaw.

DECENT LODGING OF HOP-PICKERS AND THE PICKERS OF FRUIT AND VEGETABLES.

MEMORANDUM.

Authority for making Byelaws.

Section 314 of the Public Health Act, 1875 (38 & 39 Vict. c. 55), enacts that,—

"Any local authority may, if they think fit, make byelaws for securing the decent lodging and accommodation of persons engaged in hop-picking within the district of such authority;"

and section 2 of the Public Health (Fruit Pickers Lodgings) Act, 1882 (45 & 46 Vict. c. 23), provides that section 314 of the Public Health Act, 1875—

"* * * * shall be deemed to extend to and authorise the making of byelaws for securing the decent lodging and accommodation of persons engaged in the picking of fruit and vegetables."

Local Authorities competent to make Byelaws.

It will be seen that the model byelaws for securing the decent lodging and accommodation of persons engaged in hop-picking, or in the picking of fruit and vegetables, may be adopted by any Urban or Rural District Council.

Scope of the Model Byelaws.

The model byelaws are intended to apply so as to secure the decent lodging and accommodation of persons engaged in the picking of hops, fruit, or vegetables, in cases where the tents, sheds, or other habitations in which such persons are housed, are provided by persons other than the pickers themselves (*i.e.*, where the pickers are not lodged in their own vans, tents, &c.). Where they are so lodged, the cleanliness and proper condition of their habitations may be secured by the making and enforcement of byelaws under section 9 (2) of the Housing of the Working Classes Act, 1885 (48 & 49 Vict. c. 72). See *ante*, pages 37—44.

Confirmation of the Byelaws.

Byelaws made under section 314 of the Public Health Act, 1875, and section 2 of the Public Health (Fruit Pickers Lodgings) Act, 1882, require confirmation by the Local Government Board, and should be submitted to that Board, for preliminary approval, in draft, before any steps are taken with regard to the formal adoption of the byelaws.

MODEL BYELAWS OF THE LOCAL GOVERNMENT BOARD AS TO HOP-PICKERS, FRUIT-PICKERS, ETC.

BYELAWS

MADE BY THE* FOR SECURING THE DECENT LODGING AND ACCOMMODATION OF PERSONS ENGAGED IN HOP-PICKING OR IN THE PICKING OF FRUIT AND VEGETABLES IN THE†

Interpretation.

1. Throughout these byelaws the expression "the Council" means the* . Interpretation.

Decent lodging.

2. Every person providing any tent, shed, barn, hopper-house, building, or other habitation for the lodging of persons engaged in hop-picking or in the picking of fruit and vegetables, and not being a building ordinarily occupied as a dwelling-house, or for human habitation, shall comply with the following conditions :—

(i.) He shall cause such habitation to be so constructed and maintained that it may be clean, dry, and weather-proof at all times when used for the lodging of such persons. Habitations to be clean and dry.

(ii.) He shall cause such habitation in every case to be properly ventilated, and sufficiently lighted. Ventilation and lighting.

(iii.) He shall not cause or allow a greater number of adult persons to be received into such habitation, or any room therein, at any one time, for the purpose of sleeping therein, than may be compatible with the allowance of *sixteen square feet* at the least of available floor space in respect of each adult person. Floor space.

---

* "Mayor, aldermen, and burgesses of the borough of , acting by the Council"; *or*, "Urban [*or* Rural] District Council of ," *as the case may be.*

† *Insert name of borough or urban or rural district, or, if the byelaws are to apply to part only of a rural district,* "that portion of the Rural District of which comprises the contributory places of ," *as the case may be.*

For the purpose of the foregoing provision two children under ten years of age shall be counted as one adult person.

Sleeping arrangements.

(iv.) He shall cause every room or part of such habitation, which may be appropriated for the reception of adult persons of different sexes, to be so furnished or provided that every bed shall be properly separated from any other bed by a suitable screen or partition, of such material, construction, and size as to secure adequate privacy to the occupant or occupants of such bed.

Cooking places.

(v.) He shall provide in a safe and suitable position in, or in connection with, or adjacent to such habitation, a suitable cooking-house, or other place, properly covered or sheltered, in which fires may be safely and readily lighted, and food may be properly cooked, and clothes and other articles may be properly dried.

He shall cause such cooking-house or place to be so constructed that for every *fifteen persons* authorised to be received in such habitation a separate fireplace or separate accommodation for the cooking of food, and the drying of clothes and other articles, may be provided.

Water supply.

(vi.) He shall (where the same is not otherwise readily available) provide in or upon or in connection with such habitation, or in some suitable place readily accessible therefrom, such a supply of good and wholesome water as will, at all times, suffice for the reasonable requirements, whether for drinking, cooking, or washing, of the several persons received and lodged in such habitation.

Straw, etc., for bedding.

(vii.) He shall provide for every person received and lodged in such habitation a sufficient supply of clean, dry straw, or other clean, dry, and suitable bedding.

He shall cause such straw or other bedding to be changed or properly cleansed, from time to time, as often as occasion may require.

Cleansing of habitations.

(viii.) He shall cause every part of the interior of such habitation, and of any cooking-house, privy, or other premises in connection therewith, to be thoroughly cleansed immediately before any person shall be received to lodge therein, and from time to time, as occasion may require, while the lodgers are retained therein.

He shall cause the walls and ceilings of every room constructed of brick, stone, iron, concrete, wood, earth, or plaster to be well and sufficiently lime-washed at least *once in every year,* and he shall from time to time cause all accumulations or deposits of filth or any offensive or noxious matter to be removed from such habitation or premises, and from the land immediately surrounding such habitation or premises, or adjoining thereto.

(ix.) He shall provide, in a suitable position in connection with such habitation, a sufficient number of water-closets, earthclosets or privies, properly constructed, for the separate use of each sex. **Privy accommodation.**

Penalties.

3. Every person who shall offend against any of the foregoing byelaws shall be liable for every such offence to a penalty of *five pounds,* and in the case of a continuing offence to a further penalty of *forty shillings* for each day after written notice of the offence from the Council. **Penalties.**

Provided, nevertheless, that the justices or court before whom any complaint may be made or any proceedings may be taken in respect of any such offence may, if they think fit, adjudge the payment as a penalty of any sum less than the full amount of the penalty imposed by this byelaw.

*Repeal of Byelaws.**

4. From and after the date of the confirmation of these byelaws, the byelaws for securing the decent lodging and accommodation of persons engaged in hop-picking, or in the picking of fruit and vegetables, which were made by the on the day of in the year one thousand eight hundred and , and which were confirmed by the Local Government Board on the day of in the year one thousand eight hundred and , shall be repealed. **Repeal.**

* *If this clause is not included in the series submitted to the Local Government Board for approval, it should be stated whether or not there are any byelaws in force upon the subject.*

PART III.

PUBLIC FOOD SUPPLY.

PUBLIC SLAUGHTER-HOUSES.

MEMORANDUM.

Authority for making Byelaws.

It is enacted by section 169 of the Public Health Act, 1875 (38 & 39 Vict. c. 55), that—

"Any Urban Authority may, if they think fit, provide slaughter-houses, and they shall make byelaws with respect to the management and charges for the use of any slaughter-houses so provided."

* * * * *

"Nothing in this section shall prejudice or affect any rights, powers, or privileges of any persons incorporated by any local Act passed before the passing of the Public Health Act, 1848, for the purpose of making and maintaining slaughter-houses."

The same section (second paragraph), by incorporating sections 125 to 131 of the Towns Improvement Clauses Act, 1847 (10 & 11 Vict. c. 34), authorises the making of certain other byelaws with respect to slaughter-houses; but these apply only to slaughter-houses not provided by the Urban Authority, and the matters which can be dealt with by such byelaws are specified in section 128 of the Act of 1847. Byelaws with respect to "the management" of public slaughter-houses, however, may include other matters; and the annexed series of model byelaws has been drawn so as to give every Local Authority who may adopt them the full benefit of the terms of the enactment under which they will be made.

Confirmation of the Byelaws.

Byelaws such as those here suggested require confirmation by the Local Government Board. A draft of the clauses should be submitted to them for their preliminary approval, before any steps are taken with regard to the formal adoption of the byelaws.

Recommendations of Royal Commission on Tuberculosis.

The Royal Commission on Tuberculosis, in their Report [Parliamentary Paper, C.—8824] express themselves as holding "the strongest opinion in favour of public over private slaughter-houses" as contributing to efficiency and uniformity of meat-inspection (pp. 8, 10). They believe, they say, "that the use of public slaughter-houses in populous places, to the exclusion of all private ones, is a necessary preliminary to a uniform and equitable system of meat inspection" (p. 10). "Naturally, those who have vested interests in private slaughter-houses object to interference with their property. But instances might be given in which these objections have been satisfactorily overcome" (*ib.*). The Commissioners recommend that, as regards "all towns and municipal boroughs in England and Wales, and in Ireland, powers be conferred on the Local Authorities similar to those conferred on Scottish corporations and municipalities by the Burgh Police (Scotland) Act, 1892, viz. :—(*a.*) When the Local Authority in any town or Urban District in England and Wales and Ireland have provided a public slaughter-house, power be conferred on them to declare that no other place within the town or borough shall be used for slaughtering, except that a period of three years be allowed to the owners of existing registered slaughter-houses to apply their premises to other purposes. The term of three years to date, in those places where adequate public slaughter-houses already exist, from the public announcement by the Local Authority that the use of such public slaughter-houses is obligatory, or in those places where public slaughter-houses have not been erected, from the public announcement by the Local Authority that tenders for their erection have been accepted. (*b.*) That Local Authorities be empowered to require all meat slaughtered elsewhere than in a public slaughter-house, and brought into the district for sale, to be taken to a place or places where such meat may be inspected; and that Local Authorities be empowered to make a charge to cover the reasonable expenses attendant on such inspection. (*c.*) That when a public slaughter-house has been established, inspectors shall be engaged to inspect all animals immediately after slaughter, and stamp the joints of all carcases passed as sound." The Commissioners admit that the case of rural districts presents some difficulty. But lest there should be a dangerous tendency to send unwholesome animals to be slaughtered and sold in small villages where they would escape detection, a system of inspection in such districts, to be administered by the county councils, is recommended.

Before the views of the Commissioners as regards meat inspection can be fully carried into effect, further legislation will be necessary. But in the meantime, the power of providing slaughter-houses conferred by the first paragraph of section 169 of the Public Health Act, 1875, is extremely valuable; and the matter has so important a bearing upon the public food supply, that it is to be hoped Local Authorities in future will be less slow to avail themselves of this power. As regards the diminution of the number of private slaughter-houses, the provisions of section 29 of the Public Health Acts Amendment Act, 1890, are important; as these enable the Local Authority to limit the time during which licences for the use and occupation of slaughter-houses shall remain in force. The time limited may be any period not less than twelve months.

Qualification of meat inspectors.

"Under section 116 of the Public Health Act, 1875 (38 & 39 Vict. c. 55), any medical officer of health or inspector of nuisances may at all reasonable times inspect and examine any animal, carcase or meat exposed for sale, or deposited in any place for the purpose of sale, or of preparation for sale, and intended for the food of man. If the animal, carcase or meat appears to the medical officer of health or inspector of nuisances to be diseased or unsound or unwholesome, or unfit for the food of man, he may seize and carry it away in order to have it dealt with by a Justice." (*Circular Letters of Local Government Board to Town Councils and Urban and Rural District Councils, dated March 11th,* 1899.) "Under section 131 of the Towns Improvement Clauses Act, 1847 (10 & 11 Vict. c. 34), which is incorporated with the Public Health Act, 1875, the inspector of nuisances, the officer of health or any other officer appointed by the Council for the purpose, may at all reasonable times enter and inspect any building or place within the district kept or used for the sale of butcher's meat or for slaughtering cattle, and examine whether any cattle or the carcase of any cattle is deposited there. If the officer finds any cattle or the carcase or part of the carcase of any beast which appears unfit for the food of man, he may seize and carry the same before a Justice, so that it may be dealt with.

"Moreover, where the Council are in a position to establish or regulate markets under section 167 of the Public Health Act, any inspector of provisions appointed by them may, under section 15 of the Markets and Fairs Clauses Act, 1847 (10 & 11 Vict. c. 14), which is incorporated with the Public Health Act, seize any unwholesome meat sold or exposed for sale in the market and carry the same before a Justice to be dealt with." (*Circular Letters of Local Government Board to Town Councils and Urban District Councils, dated as above.*)

"The Royal Commission on Tuberculosis considered that meat inspectors should possess certain qualifications. Their recommendation on the subject will be found on page 21 of their Report, and is as follows :—

"'We recommend that in future no person be permitted to act as a meat inspector until he has passed a qualifying examination, before such authority as may be prescribed by the Local Government Board (or Board of Agriculture), on the following subjects :—

"'(*a.*) The law of meat inspection, and such byelaws, regulations, etc., as may be in force at the time he presents himself for examination.

"'(*b.*) The names and situations of the organs of the body.

"'(*c.*) Signs of health and disease in animals destined for food, both when alive and after slaughter.

"'(*d.*) The appearance and character of fresh meat, organs, fat, and blood, and the conditions rendering them, or preparations from them, fit or unfit for human food.'

"At present a person cannot be required to pass a qualifying examination of the kind referred to before he acts as a meat inspector; but it appears to the Board that, in the case of a borough or urban district, where the work connected with the proper discharge of the duty of meat inspection is sufficient to justify the appointment of a separate officer for the purpose, it is very desirable that such an appointment should be made, and that the Council should satisfy themselves that the person appointed possesses adequate knowledge of the subjects mentioned in the recommendation of the Royal Commission.

"In the smaller districts, where the work of meat inspection is not sufficient to render necessary the appointment of a separate officer, the Board consider that regard should be had to these qualifications in making future appointments to the office of Inspector of Nuisances." (*Circular Letters above referred to.*)

Instructions to meat inspectors with regard to tuberculosis in animals intended for food.

"The Royal Commission recommended that the Board should 'be empowered to issue instructions from time to time for the guidance of meat inspectors, prescribing the degree of tubercular disease which, in the opinion of the Board, should cause a carcase, or part thereof, to be seized.

"'Pending the issue of such instructions we are of opinion that the following principles should be observed in the inspection of tuberculous carcases of cattle:

"'(*a.*) When there is miliary tuberculosis of both lungs - - - - "'(*b.*) When tuberculous lesions are present on the pleura and peritoneum - - - - "'(*c.*) When tuberculous lesions are present in the muscular system or in the lymphatic glands embedded in or between the muscles - - - - - "'(*d.*) When tuberculous lesions exist in any part of an emaciated carcase - - - - -	The entire carcase and all the organs may be seized.
"'(*a.*) When the lesions are confined to the lungs and the thoracic lymphatic glands - - - "'(*b.*) When the lesions are confined to the liver - - - - - "'(*c.*) When the lesions are confined to the pharyngeal lymphatic glands - - - - - "'(*d.*) When the lesions are confined to any combination of the foregoing, but are collectively small in extent - - - -	The carcase, if otherwise healthy, shall not be condemned, but every part of it containing tuberculous lesions shall be seized.

"'In view of the greater tendency to generalisation of tuberculosis in the pig, we consider that the presence of tubercular deposit in any degree should involve seizure of the whole carcase and of the organs.

"'In respect of foreign dead meat, seizure shall ensue in every case where the pleura have been stripped.'

"The Board do not consider it necessary, at present, that anything should be added to these Instructions, or that they should be modified, and the Board think that the Council should direct those of their officers who are employed as meat inspectors to act in accordance with the principles thus laid down.

"The Board may at the same time draw attention to Article 19 (7) of their General Order of the 23rd March, 1891, with respect to the duties of an Inspector of Nuisances in relation to the inspection and seizure of meat. They may point out that where an Inspector of Nuisances is appointed under that Order, or under any Order superseded by that Order, he is required by the Article, in any case of doubt arising under it, to report the matter to the Medical Officer of Health with the view of obtaining his advice thereon. The Board think it desirable that any such inspector of nuisances should be reminded of this provision." (*Circular Letters of Local Government Board to Town Councils and Urban and Rural District Councils, dated May* 11*th*, 1899.)

Where Local Authorities license slaughter-houses.

Byelaws on this subject are contained in Model Byelaws, vol. i., pp. 247 *et seq.*

PUBLIC SLAUGHTER-HOUSES.

BYELAWS

MADE BY THE* WITH RESPECT TO THE MANAGEMENT AND CHARGES FOR THE USE OF THE SLAUGHTER-HOUSES PROVIDED BY † .

Interpretation of terms.

1. Throughout these byelaws the following words and expressions shall have the meanings hereinafter respectively assigned to them, that is to say,— Interpretation.

"Council" means the* .

"The slaughter-houses" means the slaughter-houses provided by the Council;

"Beast" means a bull, bullock, ox, cow, heifer, steer or calf;

"Animal" means any beast or other animal;

"Superintendent" means a person appointed by the Council to superintend and have the care of the slaughter-houses or of any part thereof.

With respect to the management of the slaughter-houses.

2. The slaughter-houses shall for the purpose of the admission of animals be opened on every day, not being Sunday, Good Friday, or Christmas Day, at o'clock in the morning, and shall be closed at o'clock in the evening, except on Saturday, when they shall be closed at o'clock in the afternoon. Times of opening and closing.

3. A person not being an officer or servant of the Council shall not enter or remain in the slaughter-houses except for the purpose of slaughtering or of supplying food and water to any animal therein, or of preparing any carcase for sale, or otherwise for some lawful purpose connected with the slaughter-houses. Persons authorised to be in slaughter-houses.

---

* "Mayor, aldermen, and burgesses of the borough of , acting by the Council"; *or,* "Urban District Council of ," *as the case may be.*

† "The corporation of the said borough," *or* "the said council," *according to the circumstances.*

Applications for use of slaughter-houses.

4. Every person who may desire to use the slaughter-houses for the purpose of slaughtering shall make application, in writing, to the superintendent, and permission to use the slaughter-houses shall be given to the several persons so applying, in the order in which such applications are received.

Orders of superintendent to be obeyed.

5. Every person using the slaughter-houses shall obey all reasonable orders given to him by the superintendent.

Animals not intended for human food,

6. A person shall not bring into the slaughter-houses any animal which is not intended for food of man, and in particular he shall not bring any dog into the slaughter-houses.

and dead animals, prohibited.

7. A person shall not bring into the slaughter-houses the carcase or any part of the carcase of any animal already dead or slaughtered.

Diseased animals.

8. Every person bringing into the slaughter-houses any animal which is, or is suspected of being diseased, shall take the same to the lair set apart for the reception of such animals, and shall immediately inform the superintendent of his having done so.

9. Every person slaughtering in the slaughter-houses any animal which, after the slaughtering of such animal, is found or suspected to have been diseased, shall take the same to the place set apart for the reception of the carcases of diseased animals, and shall immediately inform the superintendent of his having done so.

Animals to be properly secured.

10. Every person who shall bring or cause to be brought into the slaughter-houses any beast, shall cause such beast to be securely tied to the tying irons in a byre assigned for the purpose; and

Every person who shall bring or cause to be brought into the slaughter-houses any sheep, lamb, or goat, shall cause such sheep, lamb, or goat to be properly penned in a lair assigned for the purpose; and

Every person who shall bring or cause to be brought into the slaughter-houses any pig shall cause such pig to be properly secured in a piggery assigned for the purpose.

Bedding of lairs.

11. Every person using any lair in the slaughter-houses shall provide the same with proper and sufficient bedding, and shall remove and renew such bedding from time to time as often as may be necessary.

12. A person being the owner, or a person for the time being in charge of any animal brought into the slaughter-houses shall not cause or suffer such animal to be without food for more than *twenty-four hours* or without a sufficient quantity of wholesome water.

Sufficient food and water to be supplied.

13. A person being the owner, or a person in charge of any animal brought into the slaughter-houses for the purpose of being slaughtered and which may require to be supplied with food and water, shall supply such animal or cause it to be supplied with food and water on every day, except Sunday, between o'clock in the morning and o'clock in the evening.

Hours for feeding animals.

He shall on Sunday supply any such animal or cause it to be supplied with food and water between and o'clock in the morning, or and o'clock in the evening.

14. A person shall not cause or suffer any animal which may have been brought into the slaughter-houses for the purpose of being slaughtered to be taken out alive.

Animals not to be taken out of slaughter-houses alive.

15. A person shall not slaughter any animal in such a situation as will interfere with the slaughtering of any beast.

Slaughter of beasts not to be interfered with.

16. A person shall not slaughter, or attempt to slaughter, any animal in any part of the slaughter-houses except in such part as shall be from time to time assigned by the Council for the slaughter of animals of the same class or kind.

Animals to be slaughtered only in places assigned,

17. A person shall not in the slaughter-houses slaughter more than two beasts in succession if any other person is waiting to slaughter any animal.

and not more than two beasts in succession.

18. Every person who shall be about to slaughter or to assist in the slaughtering of any beast shall cause the head of such beast to be securely fastened so as to enable such beast to be slaughtered with as little pain or suffering as practicable, and shall in the process of slaughtering use such instruments and appliances, and adopt such methods of slaughtering, and otherwise take such precautions, as may be requisite to secure the infliction of as little pain or suffering as practicable.

Prevention of unnecessary pain and suffering.

Use of blood dishes.

19. Every person who shall slaughter or assist in the slaughtering of any animal in the slaughter-houses shall carefully collect all the blood flowing from the animal in a blood dish, and shall place the same in some part of the slaughter-houses where it will be secure until removed.

Deposit of refuse in receptacles provided.

20. A person shall not deposit any offal, blood, manure, garbage, or refuse in any place in the slaughter-houses except in a receptacle provided for the purpose; and

Removal of offal, etc.

Every person who shall slaughter or assist in the slaughtering of any animal in the slaughter-houses, shall remove all offal, blood, manure, garbage, or refuse from the slaughter-houses immediately after the completion of the slaughtering of such animal, and shall not throw or put, or permit to be thrown or put, or to flow into any drain of the slaughter-houses, any offal, blood, manure, or garbage from such slaughtering.

Matters not to be permitted to flow into drains.

Cleansing of place of slaughter, and articles used in slaughtering and dressing.

21. Every person using the slaughter-houses shall cause every part of the floor, or pavement of such slaughter-houses, and every part of the internal surface of every wall thereof, on which any blood or liquid refuse or filth may have been spilt or splashed, or with which any offensive or noxious matter may have been brought in contact during the process of slaughtering or dressing any animal, and every article or appliance which may have been used by him in slaughtering or dressing any animal, to be thoroughly washed and cleansed within *one hour* after the completion of such slaughtering and dressing. He shall not scrape or cause to be scraped any bench, block, table, or stool provided by the Council for use in or in connection with the slaughtering or dressing of animals in the slaughter-houses.

Removal of hide or skin and fat.

22. Every person who shall slaughter, or cause to be slaughtered, any animal in the slaughter-houses shall cause the hide or skin and fat of such animal to be removed from the slaughter-houses within * hours from the completion of the slaughtering of such animal.

Carcases not to be left in slaughter-houses.

23. A person shall not leave the carcase of any animal or any part thereof in the slaughter-houses for a longer period than † hours.

---

* "Eighteen" *to* "twenty-four hours" *may be suggested.*

† "Twenty-four hours" *may be suggested.*

24. A person who shall have slaughtered any pig in the slaughter-houses shall not use or attempt to use any scalding tank therein before any person who shall previously have slaughtered any pig therein. Use of scalding tanks in turn.

25. A person shall not keep any pig in any scalding tank or upon any block for any longer time than may be reasonably necessary for the completion of the several processes in connection with the dressing of the carcase of such pig. Scalding tank, etc. not to be used for an unreasonable time.

26. A person shall not use any undue quantity of hot water supplied for use in the slaughter-houses, so as to hinder any other person from having a due proportion of such water. Undue use of hot water.

27. Every person who shall use the apparatus provided by the Council in the slaughter-houses for scalding, shall on the completion of any scalding empty the water from the tank and hang up every carcase which may have been scalded by him in the place provided for that purpose. Tank to be emptied after use.

28. A person shall not singe any pig or scrape any gut in any part of the slaughter-houses. Pig-singeing and gut-scraping prohibited.

29. Every person who shall use any water tap in the slaughter-houses, shall cause the same to be properly turned off immediately after he shall have finished using such tap. Water taps to be turned off.

30. A person shall not carelessly or negligently injure, or destroy any of the plant, gear, or apparatus belonging to, or provided for use in the slaughter-houses, but shall, in the use of the slaughter-houses, and of any plant, gear or apparatus so provided, use reasonable and proper care. Damage to plant, etc.

31. A person shall not use any article provided by the Council for use in or in connection with the slaughtering or dressing of animals in the slaughter-houses except for the purposes for which the same respectively are intended to be used, or use the same for an undue length of time so as to hinder any other person from the use thereof in due order. Improper use and removal of plant forbidden.

He shall not remove from the slaughter-houses any utensil, article, gear, or apparatus provided by the Council for use therein.

32. A person shall not obstruct or hinder any other person in the proper use of the slaughter-houses, or of any utensil, Obstruction.

article, gear, or apparatus provided by the Council for use therein.

Disturbance and interruption.

33. A person shall not by any disorderly or improper conduct, disturb or interrupt any other person in the proper use of the slaughter-houses, or of any utensil, article, gear, or apparatus provided by the Council for use therein.

Regulation of carts, etc.

34. A person resorting to the slaughter-houses in charge of any cart or other vehicle shall not station such cart or vehicle in the slaughter-houses in such a manner as to hinder any other cart or vehicle in arriving at or departing from the slaughter-houses, or wilfully and improperly station such cart or vehicle so as to occupy a position in which the person in charge of any other cart or vehicle would, by priority of arrival, have prior claim to place such last-mentioned cart or vehicle.

Bad language. Drunkenness.

35. A person shall not in the slaughter-houses use any indecent or obscene language, or enter or remain therein in a state of intoxication.

Intoxicating liquors.

36. A person shall not, except in any case of illness, bring any malt or spirituous liquors into the slaughter-houses.

With respect to the charges for the use of the slaughter-houses.

Charges for use of slaughter-houses.

37. The charges to be paid for the use of the slaughter-houses shall be the sums specified in the following table:

Table of charges for use of the slaughter-houses.

PART I.

For slaughtering, including use of lairs for any period not exceeding* hours, and of all necessary utensils, articles, gear, apparatus and conveniences,—

	s.	d.
* For every bull, bullock, ox, cow, heifer, or steer - - - - - - -		
For every calf - - - - - - -		
For every sheep or lamb - - - - -		
For every pig - - - - - - -		

* *The blanks in this clause should be filled before the draft is submitted to the Local Government Board.*

PART. II.

* For use of lairs for every * hours, or part of that time, after the first * hours,—

For every bull, bullock, ox, cow, heifer or steer - - - - - - - -

For every calf, sheep, lamb, or pig - -

38. Every person who may become liable to the payment of any charge for the use of the slaughter-houses, shall pay the same before the removal from the premises of the carcase of any animal in respect of which such charge may have become due.

Provided as regards the sums specified in Part I. of the foregoing table, that the appropriate charge shall be due and payable, and shall be paid immediately upon an animal being brought into any part of the slaughter-houses.

Penalties.

39. Every person who shall offend against any of the foregoing byelaws with respect to the management of the slaughter-houses shall be liable for every such offence to a penalty of *five pounds*, and in the case of a continuing offence, to a further penalty of *forty shillings* for each day after written notice of the offence from the Council.

Provided, nevertheless, that the justices or court before whom any complaint may be made or any proceedings may be taken in respect of any such offence may, if they think fit, adjudge the payment as a penalty of any sum less than the full amount of the penalty imposed by this byelaw.

---

* *The blanks in this clause should be filled before the draft is submitted to the Local Government Board.*

DAIRIES, COWSHEDS AND MILKSHOPS.

MEMORANDUM

of the Local Government Board as to Dairies, Cowsheds and Milkshops.

Article 13 of the Dairies, Cowsheds and Milkshops Order of 1885, issued by the Privy Council in pursuance of section 34 of the Contagious Diseases (Animals) Act, 1878 (41 & 42 Vict. c. 74), provides that "a Local Authority may from time to time make regulations for the following purposes, or any of them :—

" (*a*.) For the inspection of cattle in dairies.

" (*b*.) For prescribing and regulating the lighting, ventilation, cleansing, drainage, and water-supply of dairies and cowsheds in the occupation of persons following the trade of cowkeepers or dairymen.

" (*c*.) For securing the cleanliness of milk-stores, milk-shops, and of milk-vessels used for containing milk for sale by such persons.

" (*d*.) For prescribing precautions to be taken by purveyors of milk and persons selling milk by retail against infection or contamination."

The following provisions apply to any regulations so made :—

" (1.) Every regulation shall be published by advertisement in a newspaper circulating in the District of the Local Authority.

" (2.) The Local Authority shall send to the Privy Council [now Local Government Board] a copy of every regulation made by them not less than one month before the date named in such regulation for the same to come into force.

"(3.) If at any time the Privy Council are satisfied on enquiry, with respect to any regulation, that the same is of too restrictive a character, or otherwise objectionable, and direct the revocation thereof, the same shall not come into operation, or shall thereupon cease to operate, as the case may be."

(See Article 14 of the Order.)

The expression "Local Authority" means (outside the Metropolis) the Council of any Urban or Rural District, and includes the Council of a County Borough.

By the operation of section 9 (1) of the Contagious Diseases (Animals) Act, 1886 (49 & 50 Vict. c. 32), the jurisdiction of the Privy Council under section 34 of the Contagious Diseases (Animals) Act, 1878, and the Dairies, Cowsheds, and Milkshops Order of 1885, has been transferred to the Local Government Board.

After consideration of the Report of the Royal Commission on Tuberculosis,* a model series of regulations has been prepared by the Board for the guidance of Councils in making regulations under the Order.

The model has been framed with close regard to the terms of Article 13 of the Order, which determines the matters that can be dealt with by regulation. Under other Articles of the Order Local Authorities have large powers of control over persons following or proposing to follow the trade of cowkeeper, dairyman or purveyor of milk, but in framing regulations the Board consider that the precise terms and limitations of Article 13 must be borne in mind.

It will be seen that No. 8 of the Model Regulations, which deals with the question of air space in cowsheds, does not apply to cowsheds the cows from which are habitually grazed on grass land during the greater part of the year, and, when not so grazed, are habitually turned out during a portion of each day; and it is obvious that a regulation on this subject, which might be adapted to cowsheds in towns, where the cows are kept and fed within the building, might be unsuitable for cowsheds in the country where the cows are regularly grazed on grass land during the greater part of the year, and are during the rest of the year usually turned out for a portion of each day.

---

* Parliamentary Paper (C. 8824) 1898.

The Royal Commission, in their recommendations, drew a distinction between the rules which should be observed on this subject as regards cowsheds situate in populous and those situate in non-populous places, but no indication was given as to the means by which this distinction was to be made. The clauses suggested by the Board, however, seek to give effect to the recommendations of the Commissioners by recognising that which probably constitutes the chief difference between cowsheds in towns and cowsheds in the country, viz.: that in the one case cows are kept entirely, or as a rule, indoors, and that in the other cows are usually turned out to graze, and by distinguishing between the two classes of cases.

It will be noticed that No. 4 of the Model Regulations which provides that every cowkeeper must cause every cowshed in his occupation to be sufficiently ventilated, and for this purpose to be provided with a sufficient number of openings into the external air to keep the air in the cowshed in a wholesome condition, applies in both classes of cases.

For the purpose of enforcing any Orders made under section 34 of the Contagious Diseases (Animals) Act, 1878, and any Regulations made thereunder, section 9 (4) of the Contagious Diseases (Animals) Act, 1886, provides that,—

> "The Local Authority and their officers, for the purpose of enforcing the said Orders and any regulations made thereunder, shall have the same right to be admitted to any premises as the Local Authority, within the meaning of the Public Health Act, 1875, and their officers have, under Section 102 of that Act, for the purpose of examining as to the existence of any nuisance thereon; and if such admission is refused the like proceedings may be taken, with the like incidents and consequences as to orders for admission, penalties, costs, expenses, and otherwise, as in the case of a refusal to admit to premises for any of the purposes of the said section one hundred and two, . . .

> "Provided that nothing in this section shall authorise any person, except with the permission of the Local Authority . . . to enter any cowshed or other place in which an animal affected with any disease is kept, and which is situate in a place declared to be infected with such disease."

The terms of Section 102 of the Public Health Act, 1875 (38 & 39 Vict. c. 55), are as follows :—

"The Local Authority, or any of their officers, shall be admitted into any premises for the purpose of examining as to the existence of any nuisance thereon, . . . at any time between the hours of nine in the forenoon and six in the afternoon; or in the case of a nuisance arising in respect of any business, then at any hour when such business is in progress or is usually carried on.

* * * * * *

"If admission to premises for any of the purposes of this section is refused, any justice on complaint thereof on oath by any officer of the Local Authority (made after reasonable notice in writing of the intention to make the same has been given to the person having custody of the premises), may, by order under his hand, require the person having custody of the premises to admit the Local Authority, or their officer, into the premises during the hours aforesaid, and if no person having custody of the premises can be found, the justice shall, on oath made before him of that fact, by order under his hand authorise the Local Authority or any of their officers to enter such premises during the hours aforesaid."

* * * * * *

As to the consequences of disobedience to an order of justices for admission of the Local Authority or any of their officers, and the costs and expenses connected with the order, attention may be directed to sections 103 and 104 of the Act of 1875.

With regard to penalties for offences against the Regulations, section 9 (5) of the Contagious Diseases (Animals) Act, 1886, provides that,—

"The like penalties for offences against . . . regulations made for the purposes of section 34 of the [Contagious Diseases (Animals) Act, 1878], as amended by this section, may be imposed by the . . . Local Authority making the same, and such offences may be prosecuted and penalties recovered in a summary manner, and subject to the like provisions, as if such . . . regulations were byelaws of a Local Authority under the Public Health Act, 1875, . . ."

In connection with this enactment, reference may be made to sections 183 and 251 to 254 (both inclusive) of the Act of 1875.

The Board's confirmation of any regulations which may be made by the Council will not be required, but if at any time the Board are satisfied on enquiry with respect to any regulation that the same is of too restrictive a character, or otherwise objectionable, they may direct its revocation (see Article 14 (3) of the Order of 1885); and the Board suggest that the draft of any regulations which the Council may propose to make should be sent to them for consideration before the regulations are formally adopted. Forms for this purpose with wide margin will be supplied by the Board on application.

S. B. Provis,
Secretary.

Local Government Board,
10th June, 1899.

---

*Circular Letter of the Local Government Board as to the Dairies, Cowsheds and Milkshops Order of 1885, and the Report of the Royal Commission on Tuberculosis.**

Local Government Board,
Whitehall, S.W.,
11th March, 1899.

Sir,

I am directed by the Local Government Board to advert to (1) the Dairies, Cowsheds and Milkshops Order of 1885, and (2) the Report made last year by the Royal Commission on Tuberculosis, and especially to the paragraphs in that Report which relate (*a*) to Milk, (*b*) to the qualifications of Meat Inspectors, and (*c*) to the principles which should be observed as regards the seizure of tuberculous meat intended for the food of man.

Dairies, Cowsheds and Milkshops Order.

The Council are empowered by Article 13 of the Dairies, Cowsheds and Milkshops Order of 1885 to make regulations for the following purposes, or any of them :—

(*a*.) For the inspection of cattle in dairies.

---

* This circular letter was addressed to the Councils of Boroughs and Urban Districts. A similar circular (omitting the paragraphs indicated in the following pages) was sent by the Board on the same day to Rural District Councils.

(*b.*) For prescribing and regulating the lighting, ventilation, cleansing, drainage and water supply of dairies and cowsheds in the occupation of persons following the trade of cowkeepers or dairymen.

(*c.*) For securing the cleanliness of milk-stores, milk-shops, and of milk-vessels used for containing milk for sale by such persons.

(*d.*) For prescribing precautions to be taken by purveyors of milk and persons selling milk by retail against infection or contamination.

Representations have been made to the Board to the effect that it would be desirable that they should issue model regulations for the guidance of Councils in making regulations under this Article, but they have deferred doing so pending the Report of the Royal Commission on Tuberculosis.

The Report having been made, the Board have caused some model regulations to be prepared, and two copies of them are enclosed.

It will be observed that No. 8 of the regulations, which deals with the question of air space in cowsheds, does not apply to cowsheds the cows from which are habitually grazed on grass land during the greater part of the year, and, when not so grazed, are habitually turned out during a portion of each day, and it is obvious that a regulation on this subject which might be adapted to cowsheds in towns, where the cows are kept and fed within the building, might be unsuitable for cowsheds in the country where the cows are regularly grazed on grass land during the greater part of the year, and are during the rest of the year usually turned out for a portion of each day.

The Royal Commission, in their recommendations, drew a distinction between the rules which should be observed on this subject as regards cowsheds situate in populous and those situate in non-populous places, but no indication was given as to the means by which this distinction was to be made. It is clear that it could not be accomplished by any test of population or by adopting the geographical limits of urban and rural districts without creating anomalies which would be indefensible.

Neither is it easy to see how the distinction can be carried out except upon the plan suggested by the Board, which seeks to give effect to the chief difference between cowsheds in towns and cowsheds in the country, or, in other words, between the case of cows which are kept entirely or as a rule indoors, and that of cows which are usually turned out to graze.

It will be noticed that No. 4 of the Model Regulations, which provides that every cowkeeper must cause every cowshed in his occupation to be sufficiently ventilated, and for this purpose to be provided with a sufficient number of openings into the external air to keep the air in the cowshed in a wholesome condition, applies in both classes of cases.

If the Council have not already made regulations under the Order of 1885, the Board think that they should do so, and that any such regulations would with advantage be based on the model clauses. If the Council have already made regulations under the Order, the model clauses may usefully be considered in connection with any fresh regulations or amendment of the existing code which the Council may propose to make.

The Board's confirmation of any regulations which may be made by the Council will not be required, but if at any time the Board are satisfied on inquiry with respect to any regulation that the same is of too restrictive a character, or otherwise objectionable, they may direct its revocation*; and the Board suggest that the draft of any regulations which the Council may propose to make should be sent to them for consideration before the regulations are formally adopted.†

Report of the Tuberculosis Commission.—Milk.

Article 15 of the Dairies, Cowsheds and Milkshops Order of 1885 provides that if at any time disease exists among the cattle in a dairy or cowshed, or other building or place, the milk of a diseased cow therein (*a*) shall not be mixed with other milk; and (*b*) shall not be sold or used for human food.

The term "disease" in the Order is limited to those diseases which were included under the Contagious Diseases (Animals) Act, 1878, of which tuberculosis is not one, and the Royal Commission on Tuberculosis state in paragraph 39 of their Report that "the evidence abundantly shows how this fact has precluded local authorities from any attempt to deal with tuberculosis in milch cows, although they may have shown themselves alive to the danger and anxious to provide a remedy," and they express the opinion that "it is desirable that the Order should be made applicable to all diseases of the udder in cows of which the milk is offered for sale."

The Board have issued an Order to amend Article 15 of the Order of 1885 by providing that, for the purposes of paragraphs (*a*) and (*b*) of the Article, reference to disease shall include, in the case of a cow, such disease of the udder as shall be certified by a veterinary surgeon to be tubercular.‡ The Board think that it will be com-

* See Article 14 (3) of the Dairies, Cowsheds and Milkshops Order of 1885.

† Article 14 (1) of the Order of 1885 requires that "every regulation shall be published by advertisement in a newspaper circulating in the district of the local authority." The regulations should be published *in extenso*. By Article 14 (2) the Local Authority are required to "send to the [Local Government Board] a copy of every regulation made by them not less than one month before the date named in such regulation to come into force."

‡ "The Dairies, Cowsheds and Milkshops Order of 1899," dated February 7th, 1899.

petent for the Council to employ and pay a veterinary surgeon with a view of obtaining a certificate under the Article, as amended, or to appoint him as an officer for this purpose, if they think fit to do so. Two copies of the amending Order are enclosed.

Qualification of meat inspectors.

Under section 116 of the Public Health Act, 1875 (38 & 39 Vict. c. 55), any medical officer of health or inspector of nuisances may at all reasonable times inspect and examine any animal, carcase or meat exposed for sale, or deposited in any place for the purpose of sale, or of preparation for sale, and intended for the food of man. If the animal, carcase or meat appears to the medical officer of health or inspector of nuisances to be diseased or unsound or unwholesome, or unfit for the food of man, he may seize and carry it away in order to have it dealt with by a justice. [*Under section 131 of the Towns Improvement Clauses Act, 1847 (10 & 11 Vict. c. 34), which is incorporated with the Public Health Act, 1875, the inspector of nuisances, the officer of health or any other officer appointed by the Council for the purpose, may at all reasonable times enter and inspect any building or place within the district kept or used for the sale of butchers' meat or for slaughtering cattle, and examine whether any cattle or the carcase of any cattle is deposited there. If the officer finds any cattle or the carcase or part of the carcase of any beast which appears unfit for the food of man, he may seize and carry the same before a justice, so that it may be dealt with.

Moreover, where the Council are in a position to establish or regulate markets under section 167 of the Public Health Act, any inspector of provisions appointed by them may, under section 15 of the Markets and Fairs Clauses Act, 1847 (10 & 11 Vict. c. 14), which is incorporated with the Public Health Act, seize any unwholesome meat sold or exposed for sale in the market and carry the same before a justice to be dealt with.]

The Royal Commission on Tuberculosis considered that meat inspectors should possess certain qualifications. Their recommendation on the subject will be found on page 21 of their Report and is at follows :—

"We recommend that in future no person be permitted to act as a meat inspector until he has passed a qualifying examination, before such authority as may be prescribed by the Local Government Board (or Board of Agriculture), on the following subjects :—

"(*a.*) The law of meat inspection, and such byelaws, regulations, etc., as may be in force at the time he presents himself for examination.

"(*b.*) The names and situations of the organs of the body.

* The part in brackets is not included in the Circular to Rural District Councils.

"(*c.*) Signs of health and disease in animals destined for food, both when alive and after slaughter.

"(*d.*) The appearance and character of fresh meat, organs, fat, and blood, and the conditions rendering them, or preparations from them, fit or unfit for human food.

"At present a person cannot be required to pass a qualifying examination of the kind referred to before he acts as a meat inspector; [*but it appears to the Board that, in the case of a borough or urban district, where the work connected with the proper discharge of the duty of meat inspection is sufficient to justify the appointment of a separate officer for the purpose, it is very desirable that such an appointment should be made, and that the Council should satisfy themselves that the person appointed possesses adequate knowledge of the subjects mentioned in the recommendation of the Royal Commission.

"In the smaller districts, where the work of meat inspection is not sufficient to render necessary the appointment of a separate officer, the Board consider that regard should be had to these qualifications in making future appointments to the office of inspector of nuisances."†]

Instructions to meat inspectors with regard to tuberculosis in animals intended for food.

The Royal Commission recommended that the Board should "be empowered to issue instructions from time to time for the guidance of meat inspectors, prescribing the degree of tubercular disease which, in the opinion of the Board, should cause a carcase, or part thereof, to be seized.

"Pending the issue of such instructions we are of opinion that the following principles should be observed in the inspection of tuberculous carcases of cattle:

<table>
<tr><td>"(a.) When there is miliary tuberculosis of both lungs - - - - - - -</td><td rowspan="4">The entire carcase and all the organs may be seized.</td></tr>
<tr><td>"(b.) When tuberculous lesions are present on the pleura and peritoneum - - -</td></tr>
<tr><td>"(c.) When tuberculous lesions are present in the muscular system, or in the lymphatic glands embedded in or between the muscles - - - - - - -</td></tr>
<tr><td>"(d.) When tuberculous lesions exist in any part of an emaciated carcase - -</td></tr>
</table>

* The part in brackets is not included in the Circular to Rural District Councils.

† The same observation,—that regard should be had to these qualifications in making future appointments—is made by the Local Government Board in their Circular Letter to the Rural District Councils, with reference to cases where the officer will have to exercise the powers conferred on him by s. 116 of the Public Health Act, 1875.

"(*a.*) When the lesions are confined to the lungs and the thoracic lymphatic glands - "(*b.*) When the lesions are confined to the liver - - - - - - - - "(*c.*) When the lesions are confined to the pharyngeal lymphatic glands - - "(*d.*) When the lesions are confined to any combination of the foregoing, but are collectively small in extent - - -	The carcase, if otherwise healthy, shall not be condemned, but every part of it containing tuberculous lesions shall be seized.

"In view of the greater tendency to generalisation of tuberculosis in the pig, we consider that the presence of tubercular deposit in any degree should involve seizure of the whole carcase and of the organs."

"In respect of foreign dead meat, seizure shall ensue in every case where the pleura have been 'stripped.'"

The Board do not consider it necessary, at present, that anything should be added to these instructions, or that they should be modified, and the Board think that the Council should direct those of their officers who are employed as meat inspectors to act in accordance with the principles thus laid down.

The Board may at the same time draw attention to Article 19 (7) of their General Order of the 23rd March, 1891, with respect to the duties of an inspector of nuisances in relation to the inspection and seizure of meat. They may point out that where an inspector of nuisances is appointed under that Order, or under any Order superseded by that Order, he is required by the Article, in any case of doubt arising under it, to report the matter to the medical officer of health with the view of obtaining his advice thereon. The Board think it desirable that any such inspector of nuisances should be reminded of this provision.

I am, Sir,

Your obedient Servant,

S. B. Provis,

Secretary.

The Town Clerk *or* the Clerk
to the Urban District Council.

MODEL REGULATIONS OF THE LOCAL GOVERNMENT BOARD AS TO DAIRIES, COWSHEDS AND MILKSHOPS.

REGULATIONS

MADE BY THE * WITH RESPECT TO DAIRIES, COWSHEDS AND MILKSHOPS IN THE † .

Interpretation.

1. Throughout these regulations the expression "The Council" means the* , the expression "the District" means the† , the expression "Cowshed" includes any dairy in which milking cows may be kept, and the expression "Cowkeeper" means any person following the trade of a cowkeeper or dairyman who is, or is required to be, registered under the Dairies, Cowsheds and Milkshops Order of 1885.

Cowkeeper.—It will be observed that to be a cowkeeper under these regulations, a person must follow the trade of a cowkeeper or dairyman. S. was convicted under the repealed Order of 1876 of carrying on the trade of a cowkeeper without a licence. He was a gentleman farmer, keeping cows to supply his family and for amusement, and for some years had allowed some of his neighbours to get a few pints of milk when they required it. The neighbours lived a mile off. Twenty times in one period of six weeks a dairyman had got about six quarts at a time from S., but it being winter, the dairyman was short of milk. It was held that S. was in no sense a trader, and it was straining words to call him a cowkeeper because he occasionally supplied a neighbour in this way, and therefore the court quashed the conviction (*Southwell* v. *Lewis* (1881), 45 J. P. 206).

For the inspection of cattle in dairies.

2. Every occupier of a dairy wherein any cattle may be kept, and which the medical officer of health, or the inspector of nuisances, or any other officer of the Council specially authorised by them in that behalf, may visit for the purpose of inspecting cattle, and every person for the time being having the care or control of any such dairy, or of any cattle therein,

---

* "Mayor, aldermen, and burgesses of the borough of , acting by the Council"; *or*, "Urban [*or* Rural] District Council of ," *as the case may be.*

† "Borough," *or* "Urban [*or* Rural] District of ," *as the case may be.*

shall afford such medical officer of health, inspector of nuisances, or officer, all reasonable assistance that may, for the purpose of the inspection, be required by him.

For the inspection of cattle in dairies.—Section 9 (4) of the Contagious Diseases (Animals) Act, 1886 (49 & 50 Vict. c. 32), subject as therein stated, gives the Local Authority andtheir officers, for the purpose of enforcing any Order made under s. 34 of the Contagious Diseases (Animals) Act, 1878 (41 & 42 Vict. c. 74),—*e.g.*, the Dairies, Cowsheds and Milkshops Order of 1885,—and any regulations made thereunder, the same right of admission to any premises as they have under s. 102 of the Public Health Act, 1875, for the purpose of examining as to the existence of any nuisance.

For prescribing and regulating the lighting, ventilation, cleansing, drainage, and water supply of cowsheds and dairies in the occupation of persons following the trade of cowkeepers or dairymen.

Sanitary condition of dairies, etc.—In connection with regulations under Article 13 (b) of the Order of 1885, reference may be made to Articles 7 and 8 of the Order, which contain provisions as to the water supply and sanitary state of dairies and cowsheds.

Part I.

The regulations in this Part shall apply to cowsheds the cows from which are habitually grazed on grass land during the greater part of the year, and, when not so grazed, are habitually turned out during a portion of each day.

Lighting.

3. Every cowkeeper shall provide that every cowshed in his occupation shall be sufficiently lighted with windows, whether in the sides or roof thereof.

Ventilation.

4. Every cowkeeper shall cause every cowshed in his occupation to be sufficiently ventilated, and for this purpose to be provided with a sufficient number of openings into the external air to keep the air in the cowshed in a wholesome condition.

Cleansing.

5.—(1.) Every cowkeeper shall cause every part of the interior of every cowshed in his occupation to be thoroughly cleansed from time to time as often as may be necessary to secure that such cowshed shall be at all times reasonably clean and sweet.

(2.) Such person shall cause the ceiling or interior of the roof, and the walls of every cowshed in his occupation to be properly limewashed *twice* at least in every year, that is to say, once during the month of May and once during the month of October, and at such other times as may be necessary.

Provided that this requirement shall not apply to any part of such ceiling, roof, or walls, that may be properly painted, or varnished, or constructed of or covered with any material such as to render the lime-washing unsuitable or inexpedient, and that may be otherwise properly cleansed.

(3.) He shall cause the floor of every such cowshed to be thoroughly swept, and all dung and other offensive matter to be removed from such cowshed as often as may be necessary, and not less than *once* in every day.

Drainage.

6.—(1.) Every cowkeeper shall cause the drainage of every cowshed in his occupation to be so arranged that all liquid matter which may fall or be cast upon the floor may be conveyed by a suitable open channel to a drain inlet situate in the open air at a proper distance from any door or window of such cowshed, or to some other suitable place of disposal which is so situate.

(2.) He shall not cause or suffer any inlet to any drain of such cowshed to be within such cowshed.

Floor of Cowshed.—It will be seen that paragraph (1) indirectly requires that the cowshed shall be provided with an impervious floor, a matter on which the Royal Commissioners laid some stress ; for without such a floor the regulation could not be complied with.

Water supply.

7.—(1.) Every cowkeeper shall keep in, or in connection with, every cowshed in his occupation a supply of water suitable and sufficient for all such purposes as may from time to time be reasonably necessary.

(2.) He shall cause any receptacle which may be provided for such water to be emptied and thoroughly cleansed from time to time as often as may be necessary to prevent the pollution of any water that may be stored therein, and where such receptacle is used for the storage only of water he shall cause it to be properly covered and ventilated, and so placed as to be at all times readily accessible.

What a sufficient water supply includes.—The purposes indicated in paragraph (1) would include flushing, as to which the Royal Commissioners made a special recommendation.

PART II.

The regulations in Part I., and also the following regulation, shall apply to all cowsheds other than those the cows from which are habitually grazed on grass land during the greater part of the year and, when not so grazed, are habitually turned out during a portion of each day.

8. A cowkeeper shall not cause or allow any cowshed in his occupation to be occupied by a larger number of cows than will leave not less than *eight hundred feet* of air space for each cow.

Provided as follows:—

(*a.*) In calculating the air space for the purposes of this regulation, no space shall be reckoned which is more than *sixteen feet* above the floor; but if the roof or ceiling is inclined, then the mean height of the same above the floor may be taken as the height thereof for the purposes of this regulation.

(*b.*) This regulation shall not apply to any cowshed constructed and used before the date of these regulations coming into effect, until two years after that date.

Air space required.—The power given by the Contagious Diseases (Animals) Act, 1878, and the Dairies, Cowsheds and Milkshops Order of 1885, to Local Authorities to make regulations for prescribing and regulating the ventilation of dairies and cowsheds, permits a Local Authority to make regulations respecting air space in such places (*Baker* v. *Williams*, [1898] 1 Q. B. 23 ; 66 L. J. Q. B. 880 ; 77 L. T. 495 ; 62 J. P. 28 ; 14 T. L. R. 12). Accordingly a regulation which provided that "every person following the trade of a cowkeeper . . . shall not cause or suffer any greater number of cattle to be at any time kept in a building used as a . . . cowshed, than will admit of the provision of 800 cubic feet of air space for each cow," was held valid. *Ibid.* : *Wright*, J. : "If there is any hardship, section 14 of the Order of 1885, gives power to the Privy Council—and now, I presume, to the [Local Government Board]—to cancel any regulation if it is of too restrictive a character, or otherwise objectionable."

Floor space required.—The Royal Commissioners, in their Report, refer to the desirability of requiring a minimum amount of floor space for each cow in a cowshed. As the Commissioners point out, the requirement of a minimum amount of air space for each cow is mainly of value as tending to facilitate adequate movement of air; and this would be neutralised by narrow and confined stalls. Proviso (b) to clause 8 is drawn so as to give effect to this view.

When regulation comes into effect.—This is on the lines of the recommendation on page 23 of the Royal Commissioners' Report, although a longer period of grace is given in the model than was suggested in the Report.

PART III.

9. In this Part, the expression "dairy" means a dairy in which cattle are not kept.

Lighting.

10. Every cowkeeper shall provide that every dairy in his occupation shall be sufficiently lighted with windows, whether in the sides or roof thereof.

Ventilation.

11. Every cowkeeper shall cause every dairy in his occupation to be sufficiently ventilated, and for this purpose to be provided with a sufficient number of openings into the external air to keep the air in the dairy in a wholesome condition.

Cleansing.

12.—(1.) Every cowkeeper shall cause every part of the interior of every dairy in his occupation to be thoroughly cleansed from time to time as often as may be necessary to secure that such dairy shall be at all times reasonably clean and sweet.

(2.) He shall cause the floor of every such dairy to be thoroughly cleansed with water at least *once* in every day.

Drainage.

13.—(1.) Every cowkeeper shall cause the drainage of every dairy in his occupation to be so arranged that all liquid matter which may fall or be cast upon the floor may be conveyed by a suitable open channel to the outside of such dairy, and may there be received in a suitable gulley communicating with a proper and sufficient drain.

(2.) He shall not cause or suffer any inlet to any drain of such dairy to be within such dairy.

Water Supply.

14.—(1.) Every cowkeeper shall cause every dairy in his occupation to be provided with an adequate supply of good and wholesome water for the cleansing of such dairy and of any vessels that may be used therein for containing milk, and for all other reasonable and necessary purposes in connection with the use thereof.

(2.) He shall cause every cistern or other receptacle in which any such water may be stored to be properly covered and ventilated, and so placed as to be at all times readily accessible.

(3.) He shall cause every cistern or receptacle to be emptied and thoroughly cleansed from time to time as often as may be necessary to prevent the pollution of any water that may be stored therein.

For securing the cleanliness of milk-stores, milkshops, and of milk-vessels used for containing milk for sale by persons following the trade of cowkeepers or dairymen.

Cleanliness.—As to the cleanliness of milk-stores and milkshops, see also Articles 11 and 12 of the Dairies, Cowsheds, and Milkshops Order of 1885, and as to the cleanliness of milk-vessels, Arts. 8 (b) and 11 of the Order.

Cleanliness of milk-stores and milkshops.

15. Every occupier of a milk-store or milkshop shall cause every part of the interior of such milk-store or milkshop to be thoroughly cleansed from time to time as often as may be necessary to maintain such milk-store or milkshop in a thorough state of cleanliness.

Cleanliness of milk-vessels.

16.—(1.) Every cowkeeper shall from time to time as often as may be necessary cause every milk-vessel that may be used by him for containing milk for sale to be thoroughly cleansed with steam or clean boiling water, and shall otherwise take all proper precautions for the maintenance of such milk-vessel in a constant state of cleanliness.

(2.) He shall, on every occasion when any such vessel shall have been used to contain milk, or shall have been returned to him after having been out of his possession, cause such vessel to be forthwith so cleansed.

For prescribing precautions to be taken by purveyors of milk and persons selling milk by retail against infection or contamination.

17.—(1.) Every purveyor of milk or person selling milk by retail shall take all reasonable and proper precautions, in and in connection with the storage and distribution of the milk, and otherwise, to prevent the exposure of the milk to any infection or contamination.

(2.) He shall not deposit or keep any milk intended for sale—

(*a.*) in any room or place where it would be liable to become infected or contaminated by impure air, or by any offensive, noxious, or deleterious gas or substance, or by any noxious or injurious emanation, exhalation, or effluvium; or

(*b.*) in any room used as a kitchen or as a living room; or

(*c.*) in any room or building, or part of a building communicating directly by door, window, or otherwise with any room used as a sleeping room, or in which there may be any person suffering from any infectious or contagious disease, or which may have been used by any person suffering from any such disease and may not have been properly disinfected; or

(*d.*) in any room or building or part of a building in which there may be any direct inlet to any drain.

(3.) He shall not keep milk for sale, or cause or suffer any such milk to be placed in any vessel, receptacle or utensil which is not thoroughly clean.

(4.) He shall cause every vessel, receptacle or utensil used by him for containing milk for sale to be thoroughly cleansed with steam or clean boiling water after it shall have been used, and to be maintained in a constant state of cleanliness.

(5.) He shall not cause or suffer any cow belonging to him or under his care or control to be milked for the purpose of obtaining milk for sale—

(*a.*) unless, at the time of milking, the udder and teats of such cow are thoroughly clean; and

(*b.*) unless the hands of the person milking such cow, also, are thoroughly clean and free from all infection and contamination.

Prevention of contamination of milk.—See also Arts. 9—12 of the Dairies, Cowsheds, and Milkshops Order of 1885, which prescribe certain requirements to be observed with a view to preventing the contamination of milk. The provisions of the Infectious Disease (Prevention) Act, 1890 (53 & 54 Vict. c. 34), where that Act is in force, should further be borne in mind.

The case of the *London County Council* v. *Edwards*, [1898] 2 Q. B. 75; 62 J. P. 377; 67 L. J. Q. B. 648; 78 L. T. 558, may be mentioned in this connection. That case was decided under s. 29 of the regulations of the London County Council as to Dairies, Cowsheds, and Milkshops, which provides that every purveyor of milk shall, on an outbreak of infectious disease within the building or upon the premises in which he keeps milk coming to his knowledge, remove all milk for sale from such building until it has been disinfected. The respondent, a purveyor of milk, was tenant of a three-storied building, each floor of which was adapted for separate occupation, but with a central staircase common to each. He occupied the ground floor for the purpose of his business, sublet the first floor, and occupied the second floor as a residence for himself and his family. One of his children had scarlet fever in a room on the second floor. It was held that this was an outbreak of infectious disease within the building in which the respondent kept milk, and therefore, that the non-removal from the ground floor of milk for sale there was an infringement by him of the 29th regulation.

Penalties.

18. Every person who shall offend against any of the foregoing regulations shall be liable for every such offence to a penalty of *five pounds*, and in the case of a continuing offence to a further penalty of *forty shillings* for each day after written notice of the offence from the Council.

Provided, nevertheless, that the justices or court before whom any complaint may be made or any proceedings may be taken in respect of any such offence may, if they think fit, adjudge the payment as a penalty of any sum less than the full amount of the penalty imposed by this regulation.

Power to impose penalties.—Power to impose penalties for offences against the regulations is conferred by s. 9 (5) of the Contagious Diseases (Animals) Act, 1886. See page 69.

*Commencement of the Regulations.**

19. These regulations shall come into force on and after the day of 18 .

Revocation of Regulations.†

20. From and after the date on which these regulations shall come into force, all regulations heretofore made under, or having effect in pursuance of the Dairies, Cowsheds and Milkshops Order of 1885, shall, so far as the same are now in force in the district, be revoked.

---

* See Art. 14 (2) of the Dairies, Cowsheds and Milkshops Order of 1885.

† If this clause is not included in the series submitted to the Local Government for approval, it should be stated whether or not there are any regulations in force upon the subject.

PART IV.

PUBLIC CONVEYANCES.

OMNIBUSES.

MEMORANDUM.

Authority for the Byelaws.

Byelaws with respect to omnibuses may be made under section 6 of the Town Police Clauses Act, 1889 (52 & 53 Vict. c. 14), or under any similar provision contained in any local Act. The section referred to is as follows:—

"The Commissioners [Urban District Council] may from time to time make byelaws for all or any of the following purposes, that is to say:—

"For regulating the conduct of the proprietors, drivers, and conductors of omnibuses plying within the prescribed distance in their several employments, and determining whether such drivers and conductors shall wear any and what badges:

"For regulating the manner in which the number of each omnibus corresponding with the number of its licence shall be displayed:

"For regulating the number of persons to be carried by such omnibus, and in what manner such number is to be shown thereon:

"For regulating the number and securing the fitness of the animals to be allowed to draw an omnibus, and for the removal therefrom of unfit animals:

"For securing the fitness of the omnibus and the harness of the animals drawing the same:

"For fixing the stands for omnibuses and the points at which they may stop a longer time than is necessary for the taking up and setting down of passengers desirous of entering or leaving the same:

"For securing the safe custody and re-delivery of any property accidentally left in any omnibus, and fixing the charge to be made in respect thereof:

"To provide for the carrying and the lighting of proper lamps for denoting the direction in which the omnibus is proceeding, and promoting the safety and convenience of the passengers carried thereby:

"To provide for the exhibition on some conspicuous part of every omnibus of a statement in legible letters and figures of the fares to be demanded and received from the persons using or carried for hire in such omnibus:

"To prevent within the prescribed distance—

(*a.*) the owner, driver, or conductor of any omnibus, or any other person on their or his behalf, by touting, calling out, or otherwise, from importuning any person to use or to be carried for hire in such omnibus, to the annoyance of such person or of any other person:

(*b.*) the blowing of or playing upon horns or other musical instruments, or the ringing of bells, by the driver or conductor of any omnibus, or by any person travelling on or using any such omnibus.

"Provided that nothing in this Act contained shall empower the Commissioners to fix the site of the stand of any omnibus in any railway station, or in any yard adjoining or connected therewith, except with the consent of the railway company owning such site."

The term "omnibus," as used in the Act of 1889, includes:

"Every omnibus, char-à-banc, wagonette, brake, stage coach, and other carriage plying or standing for hire by or used to carry passengers at separate fares to, from, or in any part of the prescribed distance;"

but does not include—

"Any tramcar or tram carriage duly licensed under the provisions of the Tramways Act, 1870, or of any Provisional Order made thereunder and confirmed by Parliament, or under the provisions of any local Act of Parliament:

"Any carriage starting from and previously hired for the particular passengers carried at any livery stable yard (within the prescribed distance) whereat horses are stabled and carriages let for hire, the said carriage starting from the said stable yard and being bonâ fide the property of the occupier thereof, and not standing or plying for hire within the prescribed distance:

"Any omnibus belonging to or hired, or used by any railway company for conveying passengers and their luggage to or from any railway station of that company, and not standing or plying for hire within the prescribed distance:

"Any omnibus starting from outside the prescribed distance, and bringing passengers within the prescribed distance, and not standing or plying for hire within the prescribed distance."

The expression "within the prescribed distance" means within any Urban District (38 & 39 Vict. c. 55, s. 171; 52 & 53 Vict. c. 14, s. 2).

Provisions of the Town Police Clauses Acts, 1847 *and* 1889.

In connection with the making of byelaws under section 6 of the Town Police Clauses Act, 1889, it should be pointed out that section 4 of that Act makes applicable to such conveyances, and to the drivers and conductors of such conveyances, with certain modifications, many of the provisions of the Town Police Clauses Act, 1847 (10 & 11 Vict. c. 89), relating to hackney carriages, and the drivers of such carriages. The provisions in question, as so applied, relate to the licensing of omnibuses and of the drivers and conductors of omnibuses, and provide for the keeping of a register of licensed carriages, and as to the duration and custody of licences: they impose penalties for plying for hire without a licence, and for other offences, and enable the Local Authority, in certain cases, to suspend or revoke licences. The enactment in section 43 of the Act of 1847, as to the duration of licences, is in the case of omnibuses to be read in connection with section 5 of the Act of 1889, which provides that "any licence may be granted" under the former Act "to continue in force for such less period than one year as the Commissioners may think fit, and shall specify in the licence." Wherever, in the enactments applied, the term "prescribed distance" is met with, it is to be read as referring to the Urban District (38 & 39 Vict. c. 55, s. 171).

Local Authorities competent to make Byelaws.

Byelaws under section 6 of the Town Police Clauses Act, 1889, may be made by any Urban District Council, or by any Rural District Council within whose district or any part thereof, the section has been put in force by an Order of the Local Government Board under section 276 of the Public Health Act, 1875 (see section 171 of that Act, and section 2 of the Act of 1889).

Scope of the Model Byelaws.

Clauses for each of the purposes mentioned in section 6 of the Act of 1889, except for regulating in what manner the number of persons to be carried by an omnibus is to be shown thereon, are comprised in the model series annexed. This matter is not dealt with, because of the provisions in sections 51 and 52 of the Town Police Clauses Act, 1847, which are rendered applicable to omnibuses by section 4 of the Act of 1889.—The expression "conduct," as used in section 6, does not seem necessarily limited to such matters as would be included in the term "behaviour"; and it has been construed in a wider sense in framing the present series.—The term "passenger" is used in the model clauses in the same sense as it appears to be used in the section.—Model clause 7 is framed so as to require the number of an omnibus to be marked on "plates" in consequence of the provision in section 41 of the Act of 1847.

"Motor-omnibuses."

As to motor-omnibuses, see the provisions of the Locomotives on Highways Act, 1896 (59 & 60 Vict. c. 36), and the regulations made by the Local Government Board under section 5 of that Act. The regulations referred to are to have effect notwithstanding anything in any other Act, or any byelaws or regulations made thereunder.

Stands for omnibuses.

The Local Authority are not empowered to fix the site of any stand in a railway station, or in any yard adjoining or connected therewith, except with the consent of the railway company owning such site (52 & 53 Vict. c. 14, s. 6, proviso). It is to be inferred, however, that, with such consent, they may do so.

Lamps upon omnibuses.

In the case of any district where there are in force any byelaws with respect to lights upon vehicles, made by a County or Town Council under section 23 of the Municipal Corporations Act, 1882 (45 & 46 Vict. c. 50), or section 16 of the Local Government Act, 1888 (51 & 52 Vict. c. 41), the provisions of the model clauses 4 (3), 5, 16 and 17, may require modification.

Standing or plying for hire.

As to what amounts to standing or plying for hire, see Model Byelaws, vol. i., pp. 269, *et seq.*

Confirmation of the Byelaws.

Byelaws made under section 6 of the Town Police Clauses Act, 1889, require the confirmation of the Local Government Board. They should be submitted to that Board, in the first instance, in draft, for which purpose proper draft forms are issued by the publishers of this work.

OMNIBUSES.

BYELAWS

MADE BY THE* WITH RESPECT TO OMNIBUSES IN THE† .

Interpretation of terms.

Interpretation. 1. Throughout these byelaws, the following words and expressions shall have the meanings hereinafter respectively assigned to them, that is to say,—

"Council" means the* ;

"District" means the† ;

"Passenger" and "intending passenger," except where the context otherwise requires, mean respectively a passenger carried, and a passenger desirous of being carried, in an omnibus;

"Authorised stand" and "authorised stopping-point" mean respectively a stand for omnibuses fixed by, or in pursuance of these byelaws, and a point so fixed at which omnibuses may stop a longer time than is necessary for the taking up and setting down of passengers desirous of entering or leaving the same.

For regulating the conduct of the proprietors, drivers and conductors of omnibuses plying within the district in their several employments, and determining whether such drivers and conductors shall wear any and what badges.

Conduct of proprietors, drivers and conductors.—Behaviour to passengers. 2. A proprietor, driver, or conductor of an omnibus plying within the district,—

(1.) shall conduct himself in an orderly manner, and with civility and propriety towards every passenger und intending passenger;

---

* "Mayor, aldermen, and burgesses of the borough of , acting by the Council"; *or,* "Urban [*or* Rural] District Council of ," *as the case may be.*

† *Insert name of borough, or urban or rural district, or if the byelaws are to apply to part only of a rural district,* "that portion of the rural district of which comprises the contributory places of ," *as the case may be.*

(2.) shall not, without reasonable excuse, refuse or neglect to comply with any proper requirement of any passenger or intending passenger ;

(3.) shall not wilfully deceive, or refuse to inform any passenger or intending passenger as to the destination of such omnibus, or the route by which it will proceed to such destination ; Deceiving passengers.

(4.) shall not, in any public street within the district, feed, or cause, or allow to be fed any animal attached to such omnibus, otherwise than with food contained in a nose-bag or other similar receptacle suspended from the head of such animal, or with hay held in the hand of the person feeding such animal. Feeding animals.

(5.) shall not, at any time when such omnibus is plying for hire within the district, cause or suffer any part of any plate on which, in pursuance of the byelaw in that behalf,* the number of such omnibus corresponding with the number of its licence shall be displayed, to be concealed from public view, or any part of the statement of fares, which in pursuance of the byelaw in that behalf† shall be exhibited on such omnibus to be concealed from the view of any passenger, or any such plate or statement to be inverted. Concealment of number plates and statement of fares.

(6.) shall, at the end of every journey, carefully search such omnibus with a view to the discovery of any property accidentally left in or upon such omnibus: provided that this requirement shall not apply to the driver of an omnibus which has a conductor. Searching omnibus.

(7.) shall, in every case where he shall knowingly have carried in such omnibus any person afflicted with any dangerous infectious disorder, or shall have carried therein the dead body of any person, forthwith give information thereof to the inspector of nuisances. Conveyance of infected persons and dead bodies.

3. A driver or conductor of an omnibus, plying within the district,— Conduct of drivers and conductors—

(1.) shall not smoke tobacco, or other like substance, to the annoyance of any passenger ; Smoking.

---

* See clause 7, *post*. † See clause 19, *post*.

Loitering.

(2.) shall not cause such omnibus to loiter in any public thoroughfare within the district, or to stop in any such thoroughfare (except upon an authorised stand, or for a period of more than *three minutes* at an authorised stopping-point) for any longer time than is necessary for the taking up and setting down of passengers desirous of entering or leaving such omnibus;

Constables' directions, and regulations as to traffic.

(3.) shall as regards the manner of taking up or setting down of passengers desirous of entering or leaving such omnibus when such omnibus is plying for hire, or of waiting for such purpose at or near to any place of public worship, amusement or resort, within the district, comply with the directions of every constable authorised to keep order and prevent obstruction of the streets, and observe and comply with all directions, regulations, or orders lawfully given by proper authority for the regulation of traffic in the streets;

Stopping when required.

(4.) shall bring such omnibus, or cause the same to be brought to a standstill whenever, to his knowledge, any passenger shall be desirous of leaving such omnibus, and whenever any passenger shall be desirous of entering such omnibus and such omnibus is plying for hire and is not already occupied by the full number of persons authorised to be carried by such omnibus;

Over-crowding.

(5.) shall not when plying for hire cause or suffer any person to enter or mount upon such omnibus at any time when such omnibus shall be already occupied by the full number of persons authorised to be carried by such omnibus;

Luggage.

(6.) if such omnibus be of such construction as to be adapted to the conveyance of luggage, shall, when requested by any passenger or intending passenger, and when such omnibus is plying for hire, convey therein or thereon a reasonable quantity of luggage, and afford all reasonable assistance in loading and unloading any luggage conveyed in or upon such omnibus and belonging to or in the charge of such passenger or intending passenger, and shall also afford all reasonable assistance in removing such luggage to or from any door or entrance of any house, station, or place at which he may take up or set down any passenger desirous of entering or leaving such omnibus.

(7.) shall not, when any passenger shall be entering or leaving such omnibus, wilfully start such omnibus, or cause the same to be started, before such passenger shall be seated in or upon such omnibus, or shall have alighted from the same, as the case may be. Starting and re-starting.

4. A driver of an omnibus plying within the district,— Conduct of drivers—

(1.) shall, when such omnibus is plying for hire but is not actually being used for the conveyance of passengers, station such omnibus on an authorised stand (not being one already occupied by the full number of omnibuses authorised to occupy such stand), in such a manner that the head or heads of the animal or animals attached to such omnibus shall be immediately in rear of the rearmost omnibus already occupying such stand; Stationing omnibus on stand.

(2.) shall, when such omnibus shall be stationed on an authorised stand, and any omnibus next in front of such omnibus shall be drawn forward upon, or drawn off such stand, cause such omnibus to be moved forward, so that such omnibus shall fill the place which shall have been previously occupied by the omnibus so drawn forward or driven off; Drawing forward on stand.

(3.) shall, at all times when such omnibus is plying for hire, cause every lamp provided in pursuance of the byelaw in that behalf * for denoting the direction in which such omnibus is proceeding, to be kept properly trimmed and ready for lighting. Head lamps.

5. A conductor of an omnibus plying within the district, shall, at all times when such omnibus is plying for hire, cause every lamp provided in pursuance of the byelaw in that behalf † for promoting the convenience of the passengers carried by such omnibus, to be kept properly trimmed and ready for lighting. Conduct of conductors.

6. Every driver or conductor of an omnibus plying within the district shall, at all times when driving or being in attendance upon such omnibus and such omnibus is plying for hire, wear attached to his outer clothing, in such a manner as to be plainly and distinctly visible, a metal badge, which shall be provided by the Council, and on which shall be plainly and legibly marked the number of the licence granted to such Drivers and conductors' badges.

---

* See clause 17, *post*. † See clauses 17, 18, *post*.

driver or conductor, and in the case of a driver the words "Licensed Driver," and in the case of a conductor the words "Licensed Conductor."*

For regulating the manner in which the number of each omnibus corresponding with the number of its licence, shall be displayed.

Number plates.

7. Every proprietor of an omnibus plying within the district, shall cause the number of such omnibus corresponding with the number of its licence to be painted or marked, in figures not less than *five inches* in height, and of proportionate width and breadth of stroke, on a plate affixed in a conspicuous position on the outside of such omnibus, and also, in figures not less than *three inches* in height and of proportionate width and breadth of stroke, on a plate† affixed in a conspicuous position on the inside of such omnibus.

For regulating the number of persons to be carried by such omnibus.

Number of passengers.

8.—(1.) A proprietor, driver, or conductor of an omnibus plying within the district shall not cause or suffer a greater number of passengers to be carried by such omnibus at any one time than will admit of the provision for each passenger of sitting accommodation to the extent at least of *sixteen inches* from side to side, and *fifteen inches* from back to front, and also of adequate accommodation to enable every passenger to sit with ease.

(2.) Where such omnibus shall have been duly licensed by the Council subject to the condition that such omnibus shall not be used to carry inside or outside a greater number of passengers than may be specified in the licence, such proprietor, driver or conductor shall not cause or suffer to be carried in or upon such omnibus at any one time any greater number of passengers than may be so specified.

(3.) For the purposes of this byelaw two children under the age of *ten years* may be regarded as one passenger.

---

* *If words or letters indicating the name of the district or of the Local Authority are also considered to be desirable, the byelaw may further provide for the addition of such words or letters.*

† *This may be the "fare plate," if any.*

For regulating the number and securing the fitness of the animals to be allowed to draw an omnibus, and for the removal therefrom of unfit animals.

9. Every proprietor or driver of an omnibus plying within the district shall at all times when such omnibus is plying for hire comply with such of the following provisions as shall be applicable to such omnibus: Number of animals.

If such omnibus be constructed to carry more than *twelve* passengers, he shall not allow such omnibus to be drawn by less than *two* horses:

If such omnibus be constructed to carry more than *twenty-six* passengers, he shall not allow such omnibus to be drawn by less than *three* horses:

If such omnibus be constructed to carry more than* passengers, he shall not allow such omnibus to be drawn by less than *four* horses.

10. A proprietor or driver of an omnibus plying within the district shall not at any time when such omnibus is plying for hire allow to draw such omnibus any animal which is not fit to draw the same, or which is in such a condition as to expose any passenger, or any person traversing any street, to risk of injury. Fitness of animals.

In any case where an animal attached to an omnibus which is plying for hire within the district becomes unfit to draw such omnibus, such proprietor or driver shall forthwith remove such animal or cause the same to be removed therefrom. Removal of unfit animals.

For securing the fitness of the omnibus and the harness of the animals drawing the same.

11.—(1.) Every proprietor of an omnibus plying within the district shall cause the same when plying for hire to be furnished, and kept furnished,— Fitness of omnibuses.

(*a.*) with safe and convenient steps, seats, and handrails; Steps, seats, and handrails.

(*b.*) with proper battens or proper dry covering for the floor; Floor covering.

(*c.*) with sound and suitable wheels and springs, and with a sound and suitable pole or shafts; and Wheels, springs, and pole or shafts.

(*d.*) with a sufficient brake or brakes,

---

* *Insert a suitable number, taking into consideration the circumstances of the district.*

Brakes. and in all other respects to be so furnished, fitted and maintained as to secure proper cleanliness and due provision for the safety and convenience of passengers.

(2.) If such omnibus be of such construction as to be adapted to the conveyance of luggage, such proprietors shall cause the same when plying for hire to be furnished and kept furnished with adequate means of securing such luggage while being conveyed on such omnibus.

Means of securing luggage.

(3.) If such omnibus be a closed omnibus, such proprietor shall also cause the same, when plying for hire, to be furnished and kept furnished,—

Window glasses and frames.

(*a.*) with proper window glasses set in suitable frames;

Window straps.

(*b.*) with a leathern strap or other suitable means of wholly or partially raising or lowering each window which is made to open;

Means of ventilation.

(*c.*) with adequate means of ventilation without opening the side windows;

Hand straps.

(*d.*) with a sufficient number of hand straps for the reasonable convenience of passengers carried inside such omnibus; and

Communication with driver.

(*e.*) with suitable means of communication with the driver, so placed as to be readily accessible to the conductor, or to any passenger carried in or upon such omnibus.

(4.) If such omnibus be an open omnibus, or if, being a closed omnibus, it be constructed or adapted to be used for carrying passengers outside, such proprietor shall cause the same when plying for hire to be furnished and kept furnished with a sufficient number of suitable aprons, for the reasonable convenience of any passengers who may be carried outside.

Aprons for outside passengers.

(5.) If such omnibus be a covered omnibus or an omnibus constructed so as to be capable of being covered, such proprietor shall cause the roof or other covering of such omnibus, at all times when such omnibus is plying for hire, to be reasonably water-tight.

Roof or other covering.

Substantial condition of harness.

12. Every proprietor of an omnibus plying within the district shall cause the harness provided for use in connection with such omnibus when plying for hire to be suitable and sufficient in every part, and to be wholly or partially renewed from time to time, as often as may be requisite for the maintenance of such harness in a safe and proper condition.

13. Every driver of an omnibus plying within the district shall, at all times when such omnibus is plying for hire, cause every part of the harness of the animal or animals drawing such omnibus to be reasonably clean and in good order, and to be so fastened and adjusted that such animal or animals shall be properly and securely attached to such omnibus, and may be properly controlled by such driver. Cleanliness and fastening of harness.

For fixing the stands for omnibuses and the points at which they may stop a longer time than is necessary for the taking up and setting down of passengers desirous of entering or leaving the same.

14. The several places specified in the second column of the following table shall be the authorised stands for such class or description, and for such number of omnibuses as shall in each case be specified in the first and third columns respectively of such table; and Authorised stands.

The several places specified in the fourth column of such table shall in each case be the points at which omnibuses of the class or description specified in the first column may stop a longer time than is necessary for the taking up and setting down of passengers desirous of entering or leaving the same. Authorised stopping points.

Class or Description of Omnibuses.	Situation or Description of Stands.	Number of Omnibuses authorised to be placed on each Stand.	Situation or Description of Stopping Points.
(1.)	(2.)	(3.)	(4.)
Omnibuses plying between and			
Omnibuses plying between and			
Omnibuses plying between and			

Provided that any place which may hereafter be appointed by the Council, and may be indicated by a notice board affixed or set up in some conspicuous position at or near to such place, shall, in addition to or in substitution for the places specified in the foregoing table or any of them, be an authorised stand for such class or description and for such number of omnibuses, as shall be specified in such notice board, or (as the case may be) a point at which omnibuses of such class or description as shall be specified in such notice board may stop a longer time than is necessary for the taking up or setting down of passengers desirous of entering or leaving the same.

For securing the safe custody and re-delivery of any property accidentally left in any omnibus, and fixing the charge to be made in respect thereof.

Property left in omnibus.

15. Every proprietor, driver, or conductor of an omnibus plying within the district by whom any property accidentally left in such omnibus may have been found, or to whom any such property may have been delivered shall, if such property be not sooner claimed by or on behalf of the owner thereof, within *twelve hours* after such finding or delivery, deposit such property or cause the same to be deposited, in the state in which it shall have been found or received by such proprietor, driver, or conductor, at the office of the Council, in the custody of the officer for the time being in charge of such office.

Authorised charge for property left in omnibus.

16. Where any property accidentally left in any omnibus plying within the district shall have been found by or delivered to the proprietor, driver, or conductor of such omnibus, and shall by him or on his behalf have been deposited at the office of the Council as required by the foregoing byelaw, such proprietor, driver, or conductor shall be entitled in the event of the re-delivery of such property to the person appearing to be the owner thereof, to demand and receive as a charge in respect of such property a sum not exceeding *five shillings*, if the estimated value of such property be not more than *five pounds* or if the value of such property cannot readily be estimated; and if the estimated value of such property be more than *five pounds*, such proprietor, driver, or conductor shall be entitled to demand and receive as a charge in respect of such property a sum equal to *one shilling in the pound* on the estimated value of the property, but in no case more than *two pounds*.

To provide for the carrying and the lighting of proper lamps for denoting the direction in which the omnibus is proceeding and promoting the safety and convenience of the passengers carried thereby.

17. Every proprietor of an omnibus plying within the district shall provide for such omnibus at least one sufficient lamp, of such construction and so placed as, when lighted, to show a bright *white* light in the direction in which such omnibus is proceeding; and in the case of a closed omnibus, he shall provide for such omnibus at least one other lamp of such construction and so placed as, when lighted, to afford a sufficient amount of light throughout the interior of the omnibus for the reasonable convenience of the passengers carried therein. **Provision of lamps.**

18.—(1.) Every driver of an omnibus plying within the district at all times when such omnibus is plying for hire between sunset and sunrise and the public street lamps are required to be lighted, or at any time during the prevalence of such a fog as may render such light necessary, shall cause every lamp provided in pursuance of the foregoing byelaw for denoting the direction in which such omnibus is proceeding, to be properly lighted and kept lighted until such omnibus shall cease to ply for hire, or until the cessation of the cause which may have rendered such light necessary; and **Lighting of lamps.**

(2.) Every conductor, or where there is no conductor, the driver of any such omnibus shall, at any time when such light may be reasonably necessary, cause every lamp provided in pursuance of the foregoing byelaw for promoting the convenience of the passengers carried by such omnibus, to be properly lighted and kept lighted until the cessation of the cause which may have rendered such light necessary.

To provide for the exhibition on some conspicuous part of every omnibus of a statement in legible letters and figures of the fares to be demanded and received from the persons using or carried for hire in such omnibus.

19. Every proprietor of an omnibus plying within the district shall, at all times when such omnibus may be plying for hire, cause a statement in legible letters and figures of the fares to be demanded and received from the persons using or carried for hire in such omnibus, to be exhibited on a suitable **Statement of fares.**

board or plate affixed to the inside of the door, or otherwise in some conspicuous position on the inside of such omnibus.

To prevent within the district the owner, driver, or conductor of any omnibus, or any other person on their or his behalf, by touting, calling out, or otherwise, from importuning any person to use or to be carried for hire in such omnibus, to the annoyance of such person or of any other person.

Touting.

20. The owner, driver, or conductor of an omnibus plying within the district, or any other person acting on their or his behalf, shall not at any time when such omnibus shall be so plying, by touting, calling out, or otherwise, importune any person to use or to be carried for hire in such omnibus, to the annoyance of such person or of any other person.

To prevent within the district the blowing of, or playing upon, horns or other musical instruments, or the ringing of bells by the driver or conductor of any omnibus, or by any person travelling on or using any such omnibus.

Use of horns, bells, etc.

21. A driver or conductor of an omnibus plying within the district, or a person travelling on or using any such omnibus, shall not at any time when such omnibus shall be so plying, blow or play upon any horn or other musical instrument, or ring any bell not being a gong provided and fixed on such omnibus for use as a signal to the driver when such omnibus is required to start or stop.

Penalties.

Penalties.

22. Every person who shall offend against any of the foregoing byelaws shall be liable for every such offence to a penalty of *five pounds*, and in the case of a continuing offence to a further penalty of *forty shillings* for each day after written notice of the offence from the Council:

Provided nevertheless, that the justices or court before whom any complaint may be made or any proceedings may be taken in respect of any such offence may, if they think fit, adjudge the payment, as a penalty, of any sum less than the full amount of the penalty imposed by this byelaw.

TRAMWAY CARRIAGES.

MEMORANDUM.

Authority for the Rules and Regulations.

The annexed series of model clauses is designed for the use of Local Authorities making rules and regulations under section 48 of the Tramways Act, 1870 (33 & 34 Vict. c. 78). That section provides that,—

"The Local Authority shall have the like power of making and enforcing rules and regulations, and of granting licences with respect to all carriages using the tramways, and to all drivers, conductors, and other persons having charge of or using the same, and to the standings for the same, as they are for the time being entitled to make, enforce, and grant with respect to hackney carriages, and the drivers and other persons having the charge thereof, and to the standings for the same in the streets and district of or under the control of the Local Authority: Provided always, that in any district in which any of the powers aforesaid in relation to hackney carriages and the matters aforesaid in connection therewith are vested in any authority other than the Local Authority of such district, such authority shall have and may exercise the powers by this section conferred upon the Local Authority."

The powers of the Local Authority with regard to hackney carriages are defined by section 171 of the Public Health Act, 1875 (38 & 39 Vict. c. 55), and the provisions of the Town Police Clauses Act, 1847 (10 & 11 Vict. c. 89), with respect to such carriages incorporated therewith.

Scope of the Model Rules and Regulations.

The scope of these model rules and regulations must be distinguished from that of the regulations which may be made respectively by the Local Authority and by the promoters of any tramway, and their lessees, under section 46 of the

Tramways Act, 1870. The latter apply to such matters as rate of speed, distance between carriages, traffic on the road in which the tramway is laid, the prevention of nuisances, etc. The rules and regulations now suggested deal with matters similar to those in regard to which byelaws as to hackney carriages can be made under section 171 of the Public Health Act, 1875 (38 & 39 Vict. c. 55), by virtue of the incorporation of section 68 of the Town Police Clauses Act, 1847 (10 & 11 Vict. c. 89). As, however, section 48 of the Tramways Act has not the effect of incorporating certain other provisions of the Act of 1847, which apply to hackney carriages, the suggested rules and regulations extend to one or two matters which, under the general law, could not be dealt with by byelaws as regards hackney carriages. See, for example, model clauses 11 and 12.

Authorities competent to make rules and regulations.

The power to make rules and regulations, such as those comprised in the model series, pertains only to the "Local Authority," as defined by section 3 and Schedule A, Part I. of the Tramways Act, 1870. The definition includes the Council of any borough, or other urban district.

Confirmation of the Rules and Regulations.

Rules and regulations such as those now in question, when made by any Urban Authority, require the confirmation of the Local Government Board (47 Vict. c. 12). In this respect, also, they differ from the regulations which may be made under section 46 of the Tramways Act, 1870, a copy of which is merely required to be sent to the Board of Trade, and to the promoters, or the Local Authority, as the case may be, in manner specified in the section. Where rules and regulations under section 48 are proposed to be made, they should be submitted for the preliminary approval of the Local Government Board in draft.

Fares.—Fares are regulated by byelaws approved by the Board of Trade. A tramway company scheduled to their Act of Parliament distinct agreements with municipal authorities not to charge tramway passengers above a fixed fare; but they afterwards obtained legislative authority to substitute omnibuses on certain routes in lieu of the tramways, and to charge a higher fare on these routes. It was held that the company had no power to increase the fare of passengers using the tramways only (*Edinburgh Street Tramway Co.* v. *Torbain* (1877), 3 App. Cas. 58; 37 L. T. 288).

User of steam engines.—The steam engines authorised by statute to be used on tramways are not locomotives within the meaning of the Locomotives Act, 1898 (61 & 62 Vict. c. 29), and therefore do not require to be licensed as therein provided (*Bell* v. *Stockton, etc., Tramway Co.* (1887), 51 J. P. 804, decided with reference to s. 32 (now repealed) of the Highways and Locomotives (Amendment) Act, 1878).

H. was driver of a steam engine on a tramway; one of the byelaws enacting that no steam shall be emitted from the engine so as to be a reasonable ground of complaint to passengers or the public. H., as driver, was resting the engine, which was not in good repair, and he could not help emitting steam, and one passenger only when passing complained of it. It was held that H. was rightly convicted, as the byelaw was imperative, and the evidence was sufficient, though he had no *mens rea*, and one passenger only complained (*Hartley* v. *Wilkinson* (1885), 49 J. P. 726).

Liability for acts of servants.—Proceedings by a tramway company under ss. 51 and 52 of the Tramways Act, 1870 (which relate to non-payment of fares), are of a criminal character, and therefore the company are liable in an action for malicious prosecution brought by a person against whom a summons in respect of such an offence has been dismissed (*Rayson* v. *South London Tramways Co.*, [1893] 2 Q. B. 204; 62 L. J. Q. B. 593; 69 J. P. 491; 42 W. R. 21; 58 J. P. 20; 17 Cox C. C. 691; 4 R. 522).

A passenger on a tramway tendered half-a-sovereign to the conductor of the car in payment of the fare. The conductor, supposing the coin to be counterfeit, gave the passenger in charge to the police. STEPHEN, J., held, on further consideration, that the tramway company were liable in an action against them by the passenger for false imprisonment (*Furlong* v. *South London Tramways Co.* (1884), 48 J. P. 329; 1 C. & E. 316).

A tramway company gave to their conductors printed instructions in which it was ordered that, except in cases of assault, conductors were not to give passengers into custody without the authority of the inspector or timekeeper. The conductor of a car, in which the plaintiff was a passenger, detained the plaintiff, and gave her into custody on a charge of passing bad money. It was held in an action for false imprisonment against the company that as the conductor had by his printed instructions no authority to give the plaintiff into custody they were not liable (*Charleston* v. *London Tramways Co.* (1888), 36 W. R. 367; affirmed 32 S. J. 557).

A person acts illegally and wrongfully in forcing his way, when intoxicated, into a tramcar while it is in motion, and by so doing places himself in a position of peril, and the conductor in a position of difficulty. Assuming the conductor did not, under the circumstances, act with the most perfect presence of mind, but still was not guilty of vexatiousness or unnecessary violence, the tramway company is not liable for damages for negligence (*Delaney* v. *Dublin Tramways Co.* (1892), 30 L. R. Ir. 725. See also *Stevens' Case*, *post*, p. 111, as to the liability of a passenger aiding and abetting a conductor in permitting overcrowding).

Liability of passengers.—A byelaw of a tramway company, which provides that each passenger shall deliver up his ticket when required to do so or pay the fare for the distance travelled over, is a reasonable byelaw (*Heap* v. *Day* (1886), 34 W. R. 627; 51 J. P. 213). A passenger, travelling under such circumstances, who shows his ticket, but refuses to deliver it up on the ground that his journey has not terminated, is liable to the penalty prescribed by the byelaw (*ibid*). A passenger who, having paid his fare and received a ticket, inadvertently loses it, and is thus unable to deliver it up when required, is liable to be convicted if he declines to pay the fare over again (*Hanks* v. *Bridgman*, [1896] 1 Q. B. 253; 65 L. J. M. C. 41; 74 L. T. 26; 44 W. R. 285; 60 J. P. 312; 18 Cox C. C. 224).

A byelaw which provides that each passenger shall show his ticket (if any) when required so to do to the conductor, or any duly authorised servant of the company, is not unreasonable, and a passenger having paid the fare and received a ticket, is liable to be convicted if he refuses to show the ticket to an inspector of the company (*Lowe* v. *Volp*, [1896] 1 Q. B. 256; 65 L. J. M. C. 43; 74 L. T. 143; 44 W. R. 442; 60 J. P. 232; 18 Cox C. C. 253).

P. was charged by the conductor under a byelaw which provided "every passenger shall, upon demand, pay the fare legally demandable for the journey," with not paying upon demand made. The fare was demanded during the journey, and P. objected that it was not legally demanded until the completion of the journey. The company were authorised by their Act of Parliament to "make regulations for regulating the travelling in or upon any carriage belonging to them," and their Act also provided that the "tolls, etc., shall be paid to such persons, and at such places upon or near to the tramways, and in such manner and under such regulations as the company shall by notice appoint." It was held that the byelaw was authorised by the Act, that it was reasonable, and that as P. had become a passenger and was travelling upon the tramway, he was liable to pay the fare whenever it was demanded of him by the conductor (*Egginton* v. *Pearl* (1875), 33 W. R. 428).

Agreements regulating services of servants.—A conductor at the time of entering the employment of a tramway company, deposited with them the sum of 5*l.*, which, together with any wages due, was agreed to be forfeited in case of any breach of the company's rules. It was further agreed that the company's manager was to be the sole judge of whether the company was entitled to retain the whole of the deposit money and wages due, and that his certificate of the cause of retention should be binding and conclusive evidence between the parties in all courts of justice and before all stipendiary magistrates, and should bar the conductor of all right to recover under the circumstances the moneys so certified to be retained. After three months' service, the conductor was discharged from his employment, and the deposit money, as well as wages due, were certified by the manager to be forfeited for non-observance of certain rules. It was held that in the absence of fraud such certificate was binding, there being nothing in the agreement that was illegal or void (*London Tramways Co.* v. *Bailey* (1877), 3 Q. B. D. 217; 47 L. J. M. C. 3; 37 L. T. 499; 26 W. R. 494).

TRAMWAY CARRIAGES.

RULES AND REGULATIONS

MADE BY THE* WITH RESPECT TO TRAMWAY CARRIAGES, AND THE DRIVERS, CONDUCTORS, AND OTHER PERSONS HAVING CHARGE OF OR USING THE SAME, WITHIN THE† .

Interpretation of terms.

1. Throughout these rules and regulations, the following words and expressions shall have the meanings hereinafter respectively assigned to them, that is to say,— Interpretation.

"The Council" means the* ;

"The district" means the† ;

"The company" means any company authorised to construct, or any company or person licensed or entitled by contract to use, any tramway within the district;

"The tramways" means the tramways within the district, or any of them;

"Tramway carriage" means and includes every carriage using the tramways.

For regulating the conduct of the drivers, conductors, and other persons having charge of, or using the tramway carriages in their several employments, and determining whether such drivers and conductors shall wear any and what badges:

For regulating the manner in which the number of each carriage corresponding with the number of its licence shall be displayed.

---

* "Mayor, aldermen, and burgesses of the borough of , acting by the Council"; *or*, "Urban District Council of ," *as the case may be.*

† *Insert name of borough or urban district.*

For regulating the number of persons to be carried by such carriages, and in what manner such number is to be shown on such carriage, and how such carriages are to be furnished or provided.

For securing the safe custody and re-delivery of any property accidentally left in tramway carriages, and fixing the charges to be made in respect thereof.

Number of carriage, and maximum number of passengers to be shown on the carriage;

2.—(1.) The company shall cause a number corresponding with the number of the licence granted in respect of any tramway carriage, to be painted or marked at each end of such carriage, inside and outside, in figures of sufficient size and breadth, and of such a colour as to be clearly and distinctly visible and legible.

(2.) They shall also cause a statement of the maximum number of passengers authorised to be carried at any one time in the inside and on the outside respectively of such tramway carriage to be painted or marked in some suitable and conspicuous position on such carriage, inside and outside, in letters and figures of sufficient size and breadth, and of such a colour as to be clearly and distinctly visible and legible.

and to be renewed when necessary.

(3.) They shall cause such number corresponding with the number of the licence, and such statement of the maximum number of passengers to be renewed respectively from time to time, as often as may be necessary for the purpose of keeping such number and such statement clearly and distinctly visible and legible on such tramway carriage.

Number, etc. not to be obliterated or concealed.

3. A driver or conductor of a tramway carriage shall not at any time whilst the same is being used on the tramways, wilfully, carelessly, or negligently obliterate or conceal, or cause or suffer to be obliterated or concealed, any number or statement which, in pursuance of these rules and regulations, has been painted or marked on any part of such carriage.

Maximum number of passengers, how determined.

4. A conductor of a tramway carriage shall not cause or suffer to be carried in or upon such carriage, at any one time, a greater number of persons than will admit of the provision of sitting accommodation to the extent at least of *sixteen inches* from side to side, and *fifteen inches* from front to back, in respect of each person conveyed in or upon such carriage.

Provided always, that in the case of any tramway carriage which has not a conductor, the foregoing provision shall be deemed to apply to the driver.

For the purposes of this byelaw two children under the age of *twelve years* may be regarded as one person.

5. A conductor of a tramway carriage shall not cause or suffer any person, not being an officer or servant of the company, to travel on any step or platform of such carriage, or to stand either upon the roof or in the interior, or to sit upon the outside rail on the roof of such carriage. Passengers not to stand, etc.

Provided always, that in the case of any tramway carriage which has not a conductor, the foregoing provision shall be deemed to apply to the driver.

6. A conductor of a tramway carriage shall not permit any person beyond the maximum number of passengers authorised to be carried at any one time in or upon such carriage, to enter or mount, or to remain in or upon any part of such carriage. Authorised number of passengers not to be exceeded.

Provided always, that in the case of any tramway carriage which has not a conductor, the foregoing provision shall be deemed to apply to the driver.

Enforcement of the byelaws.—It has been held that it is competent for a Local Authority to make and enforce a byelaw of this kind made under s. 48 of the Tramways Act, 1870, as this one would be made (*Smith* v. *Butler* (1885), 16 Q. B. D. 349; 34 W. R. 416; 50 J. P. 260).

The assent of the lessees of the line (under s. 46) is not necessary to the validity of such byelaw (*ibid.*).

A passenger incommoded by an excessive number of passengers is entitled to prosecute a conductor for breach of the byelaw (*Badcock* v. *Sankey* (1890), 54 J. P. 564).

7. Every driver or conductor of a tramway carriage shall at all times when such carriage shall be standing or plying, or be driven for hire, wear attached to his outer clothing in such position and manner as to be at all times plainly and distinctly visible, a badge consisting of a metal plate, which shall be provided by the Council, and shall be delivered to such driver or conductor together with the licence granted to him by the Council, and on which shall be engraved, impressed, painted, or marked, in legible figures, a number corresponding with the number of the licence granted to such driver or conductor, and Drivers and conductors to wear badges.

also the words "licensed driver," or "licensed conductor," as the case may be.

Condition of carriage, and harness.

8.—(1.) The company shall cause every tramway carriage, and all the furniture and fittings thereof, and every part of the harness of the animal or animals drawing such carriage, to be reasonably clean and in good order and condition, at all times when such carriage shall be standing, or plying, or be driven for hire.

Means of ventilation.

(2.) They shall cause such carriage to be provided with adequate means of ventilation without opening the side windows.

Lamps.

(3.) They shall cause such carriage to be furnished with two or more suitable lamps, so constructed and fitted as to afford, when lighted, sufficient means of lighting the interior of such carriage, and of signalling externally, to the front and rear, the approach or position of such carriage.

Floor of carriage.

(4.) They shall cause the floor of such carriage to be covered with suitable battens, or otherwise with a suitable dry or false floor.

Means of notifying when carriage is "full."

(5.) They shall cause such carriage to be provided with a board, painted or marked with letters of sufficient size and breadth, and of such a colour as to be clearly and distinctly visible and legible, or shall otherwise cause such carriage to be provided, for use when necessary, with adequate means of notifying to any intending passengers that such carriage is "full"; and they shall also cause to be provided proper means of displaying such board, or other means of notification in a conspicuous and suitable position upon the exterior of such carriage.

Brakes.

(6.) They shall cause such carriage to be furnished with proper and sufficient brakes.

Lighting of lamps.

9.—(1.) Every conductor of a tramway carriage shall, at any time when the public street lamps are required to be lighted, or at any time during the prevalence of such a fog as may render such light necessary for the safety of other vehicles, or of foot passengers, cause the lamps provided in pursuance of the foregoing byelaw to be properly lighted, and to be kept so lighted until such carriage shall cease to use the tramways, or until the cessation of the cause which may have rendered such light necessary.

Provided that, in the case of any tramway carriage which has not a conductor, the foregoing provision shall be deemed to apply to the driver.

Notification that carriage is "full."

(2.) He shall, at any time when there shall be in and upon such carriage the maximum number of passengers authorised to be carried therein and thereon at any one time, cause the board or other means of notification that such carriage is "full" provided in pursuance of the foregoing byelaw, to be properly displayed, and to be kept so displayed until the number of passengers in and upon such carriage shall be less than the maximum number authorised to be carried.

Carrying of lamps.—Where a tramway company were convicted before justices of the breach of a regulation of the Board of Trade, made under a local Act, relative to lamps being placed and lighted in a conspicuous position on the front of a tramway engine, it was held that the regulation was not invalid as a regulation, and that its subject-matter need not have been dealt with as a byelaw; that the offence, being stated in the words of the regulation, was sufficiently described, and that the company were responsible for the personal neglect of their servant (*St. Helen's Tramway Co.* v. *Wood* (1892), 60 L. J. M. C. 141; 56 J. P. 70).

Overcrowding.—Passengers over-crowding may be convicted for aiding and abetting the conductor where he is a party to the offence (*Stevens' Case* (1898), 62 J. P. 810).

Conduct of drivers and conductors

10. Every driver and conductor of a tramway carriage shall, at all times when such carriage shall be standing or plying, or be driven for hire, conduct himself in an orderly manner, and with civility and propriety towards every person seeking to be carried, or being carried in or upon such carriage.

Refusal to carry passengers.

11. The driver or conductor of a tramway carriage shall not, without reasonable excuse, neglect or refuse, when requested by any person, to receive such person as a passenger in or upon such carriage, at any time when there shall not already be in and upon such carriage the maximum number of passengers authorised to be carried therein and thereon at any one time.

Driver not to leave carriage.

12. A driver of a tramway carriage shall not, without reasonable excuse, leave such carriage at any time when the carriage may be standing or plying for passengers to be carried for hire, or when there may be any passenger in or upon the carriage, unless there shall remain in charge of the carriage, during the absence of the driver, a person competent to have the care and control of the animal or animals attached to such carriage.

Carriages not to loiter in streets.

13. A driver or conductor of a tramway carriage shall not cause such carriage to loiter in any public street.

Property left in carriage.

14. Every driver or conductor of a tramway carriage wherein any property shall be accidentally left by any person who may have been conveyed in such carriage shall, if such property be found by or delivered to such driver or conductor, within *twenty-four hours* after such finding or delivery, carry the same, if not sooner claimed by or on behalf of the owner thereof, in the state in which the same shall have been found to the office of the Council, and shall there deposit and leave such property in the custody of the officer in charge of such office.

In the event of the re-delivery of such property to any person who shall satisfactorily prove that the same belongs to him, the driver or conductor, by whom such property may have been deposited at the office of the Council, shall be entitled to demand and receive from the person to whom such property shall have been re-delivered an amount to be determined in accordance with the following regulations:

If the estimated value of the property be not more than *five pounds*, or if the property be of such a character that the value thereof cannot readily be estimated, such driver or conductor shall be entitled to demand and receive from such person any sum not exceeding *five shillings*;

If the estimated value of the property be more than *five pounds*, such driver or conductor shall be entitled to demand and receive from such person an amount equal to *one shilling in the pound* on the estimated value of the property: Provided that in no case shall such driver or conductor be entitled to demand or receive a greater amount than *two pounds*.

Penalties.

Penalties.

15. For every offence against any of the foregoing Rules and Regulations, so far as such Rules and Regulations are applicable to the company, such company shall be liable to a penalty of *five pounds*, and in the case of a continuing offence to a further penalty of *forty shillings* for each day after written notice of the offence from the Council.

For every offence against any of the foregoing Rules and Regulations so far as such Rules and Regulations are applicable to any driver or conductor of a tramway carriage, such driver or conductor shall be liable to a penalty of *five pounds.*

Provided, nevertheless, that the justices or court before whom any complaint may be made or any proceedings may be taken in respect of any such offence, may, if they think fit, adjudge the payment, as a penalty, of any sum less than the full amount of the penalty imposed by this byelaw.

PART V.

PUBLIC RECREATION.

PLEASURE GROUNDS.

MEMORANDUM.

Authority for making Byelaws.

Section 164 of the Public Health Act, 1875 (38 & 39 Vict. c. 55), enacts that,—

"Any Urban Authority may purchase or take on lease, lay out, plant, improve, and maintain lands for the purpose of being used as public walks or pleasure grounds, and may support or contribute to the support of public walks or pleasure grounds provided by any person whomsoever.

"Any Urban Authority may make byelaws for the regulation of any such public walk or pleasure ground, and may by such byelaws provide for the removal from such public walk or pleasure ground of any person infringing any such byelaw by any officer of the Urban Authority or constable."

The power to contribute to the support of public walks or pleasure grounds is extended by section 45 of the Public Health Acts Amendment Act, 1890 (53 & 54 Vict. c. 59); and section 44 of that Act provides as follows:

(1.) An Urban Authority may on such days as they think fit (not exceeding twelve days in any one year, nor four consecutive days on any one occasion) close to the public any park or pleasure ground provided by them or any part thereof, and may grant the use of the same, either gratuitously or for payment, to any public charity or institution, or for any agricultural, horticultural, or other show, or any other public purpose, or may use the same for any such show or purpose; and the admission to the said park or pleasure ground, or such part thereof, on the days when the same shall be so closed to the public may be either with or without payment, as directed by the Urban Authority, or, with the consent of the Urban Authority, by the society or persons to whom the use of the park or pleasure ground, or such part thereof, may be granted: Provided that no such park or pleasure ground shall be closed on any Sunday or public holiday.

(2.) An Urban Authority may either themselves provide and let for hire, or may license any person to let for hire, any pleasure boats on any lake or piece of water in any such park or pleasure ground, and may make byelaws for regulating the numbering and naming of such boats, the number of persons to be carried therein, the boathouses and mooring places for the same, and for fixing rates of hire and the qualifications of boatmen, and for securing their good and orderly conduct while in charge of any boat.

Local Authorities competent to make Byelaws.

Byelaws such as those suggested in the present series may be made by an Urban District Council who have adopted Part III. of the Act of 1890 above mentioned, or by any Rural District Council within whose district, or any part thereof, section 164 of the Act of 1875, and section 44 of the later Act have been put in force by an order of the Local Government Board. Clauses 4, 5, and 6, which relate to the playing of games, and to skating and fishing, can be adopted by any Urban District Council, and by any Rural District Council who have been invested with urban powers under section 164 of the Act of 1875, irrespective of any powers which they may have under the Public Health Acts Amendment Act, 1890. The clauses as to games may be of use to some parish councils making byelaws under section 8 (1) (*d*) of the Local Government Act, 1894.

Scope of the Model Byelaws.

Clauses 2 and 3 of the model series are intended for adoption where the byelaws (if any) already in force, fix the hours for opening and closing the pleasure grounds without reference to the power of closing the ground to the public conferred by section 44 of the Act of 1890, and similar enactments in some local Acts. The next three clauses contain regulations with regard to the playing of certain games, and to skating and fishing in the pleasure ground; and the remaining clauses are for the regulation, so far as is authorised by section 44 (2) of the Act of 1890, of boating in the pleasure ground if there be any lake or piece of water therein on which boating can take place. It may be pointed out, that although section 44 (1) of the Act empowers the Local Authority to make charges, or allow charges to be made for admission, on the occasions when the pleasure ground is closed to the public, no power is given to fix or regulate the charges by means of byelaws.

Boating in the pleasure ground.

The Local Authority are empowered by section 44 of the Public Health Acts Amendment Act, 1890, to themselves provide boats and let them for hire in the pleasure ground. Where they do so byelaws as to the numbering and naming of the boats appear to be unnecessary, and even when the boats are let for hire by persons acting in pursuance of the licence of the authority under sub-section (2) of the section, the numbering and naming can equally well be made a condition of the licence. No clause on this subject, therefore, is suggested. The licensing of persons to let boats for hire is not a matter on which byelaws are authorised by section 44 of the Public Health Acts Amendment Act, 1890. A clause such as number 7, which regulates the number of persons to be carried in a pleasure boat is, in the case of the usually shallow and protected waters in public pleasure grounds, necessary rather for the convenience than the safety of the public, and as such is practically required only where boats may be let to hire at a separate charge or fare for each passenger carried. The clause is drawn accordingly. It assumes that the number of persons to be carried will be fixed by the Council by or in pursuance of the conditions of the licence. A clause (number 8) is suggested for the regulation of boat-houses and mooring-places. None of its provisions extend to acts of wilful damage, as these can be dealt with under the general law. The clauses relating to the qualifications and conduct of boatmen are intentionally drawn in somewhat general terms; but the expression "good and orderly conduct" as used in the section above mentioned is construed as meaning rather more than would be expressed by the word "behaviour." The byelaws as to conduct can only apply to the boatmen "while in charge of any boat"; but a person may be "in charge" of a boat although he may not be engaged in propelling or managing it on the water, and although the boat may not, at the time, be actually in use for hire.

Confirmation of the Byelaws.

The byelaws require confirmation by the Local Government Board. They should be submitted to the Board, in the first instance, in draft, in draft forms which can be obtained from the publishers of this work.

PLEASURE GROUNDS.

BYELAWS

MADE BY THE * WITH RESPECT TO THE PLEASURE GROUND †

Interpretation of terms.

1. Throughout these byelaws the following words and expressions shall have the meanings hereinafter respectively assigned to them, that is to say,— **Interpretation.**

"Council" means the * ;

"Pleasure ground" means † .

For the regulation of the pleasure ground.

2. Subject as hereinafter provided, the pleasure ground shall be opened at o'clock in the morning, and closed at o'clock in the evening, of every day during the months of and , and shall be opened at o'clock in the morning, and closed at o'clock in the evening of every day during the rest of the year. **Hours of opening and closing.**

Provided that this byelaw shall not be deemed to require the pleasure ground to be opened and closed at the hours hereinbefore mentioned on any day on which, in pursuance of any statutory provision in that behalf, the Council may close the pleasure ground to the public.

3. A person, other than an officer of the Council, or a person employed in the laying out, planting, improvement, or maintenance of the pleasure ground, shall not, on any day on which the pleasure ground may be open to the public, enter the pleasure ground before the time prescribed by the foregoing byelaw for the opening of the pleasure ground, or enter the same, or remain therein after the time so prescribed for the closing thereof. **Entrance during prohibited hours.**

---

* "Mayor, aldermen, and burgesses of the borough of , acting by the Council"; *or*, "Urban [*or* Rural] District Council of "; *or*, "Parish Council of the parish of ," *as the case may be.*

† *Insert a description of the pleasure ground to which the byelaws are to apply.*

Playing of games.

4. A person shall not, except as is hereinafter provided, play or take part in any game of football, golf, lawn tennis, quoits, bowls, hockey, cricket, or any other game which, by reason of the rules or manner of playing, or for the prevention of damage, danger, or discomfort to any person in the pleasure ground, may necessitate, at any time during the continuance of the game, the exclusive use by the player or players of any space in the pleasure ground:

Provided that where, by a notice or notices, which shall be affixed or set up in some conspicuous position in the pleasure ground, and at or near to each of the principal entrances thereto, the Council may from time to time set apart, for the playing of any such game or games as may be specified in such notice or notices, such space or spaces in the pleasure ground as shall be defined or described in such notice or notices, this byelaw shall not be taken to prohibit any person from playing or taking part in any game or games which may be played in such space or spaces and in accordance with the following regulations:—

Undue interference with other players.

(1.) Every person resorting to any such space for the purpose of playing or taking part in any such game shall, in making preparation for the playing of such game and in the manner of playing, use reasonable and proper care to prevent undue interference with the reasonable and proper use of such space by any other person engaged in making preparation for playing or in playing therein, or thereafter resorting to such space for the purpose of making preparation for playing or of playing therein:

Undue crowding.

(2.) A person resorting to any such space for the purpose of playing or taking part in any such game shall not begin to play at any time when such space is already occupied by such a number of players, and in such a manner as to render any addition to the number of players incompatible with the safe and convenient use of such space by the players already in occupation:

Monopolising ground.

(3.) Except in any case where the exclusive use of any such space or any part thereof may have been granted by the Council for the playing of any match, of which the occasion and character shall be such as to render expedient an extension of the time hereinafter specified, a player or company of players shall not, in making preparation for playing and in playing any game, use any part of such space for a longer time than *two hours* continuously, if, at the expiration of that time any other player or company of players, for whose use no other part of such space or no part of any other space set apart for the purpose may be available, shall make known to such first mentioned player or company of players an intention to use, for the purpose of playing, such part of such space as shall have been previously used by such player or company of players.

Special regulations as to *football.*

(4.) Every person resorting to any such space for the purpose of playing or taking part in any game of football shall observe and comply with the following conditions :—

(*a.*) Football shall not be played in the pleasure ground between the *thirtieth* day of *April*, and the *first* day of *October* in any year :

(*b.*) The goal and boundary posts necessary for the playing of any game of football shall be fixed under the direction of an officer of the Council duly appointed in that behalf :

(*c.*) No game of football shall be played or continue to be played on any day later than *a quarter of an hour* before the time fixed for closing the pleasure ground.

Special regulations as to *golf.*

(5.) Every person resorting to any such space for the purpose of playing or taking part in any game of golf, shall observe and comply with the following conditions :—

(*a.*) Golf shall not be played in the pleasure ground on any day after *ten o'clock* in the morning, and between the *thirty-first* day of *March*, and the *first* day of *October*, shall not be played in the pleasure ground after *eight o'clock* in the morning.*

Provided that nothing in this regulation shall be deemed to prohibit the practice of putting at any time in the day not later than *a quarter of an hour* before the time fixed for closing the pleasure ground.

(*b.*) A person shall not in the pleasure ground play or take part in any game of golf, after *eight o'clock* in the

* *The hours here suggested may require alteration in connection with those fixed by clause* 2.

morning, unless, during the playing of such game, and in connection therewith, a forecaddy shall be employed to carry and shall carry a red flag.

Special regulations as to *lawn tennis.*

(6.) Every person resorting to any such space for the purpose of playing or taking part in any game of lawn tennis shall observe and comply with the following conditions:—

(*a.*) Lawn tennis shall not be played in the pleasure ground between the *thirtieth* day of *September* and the *first* day of *May*.

(*b.*) The net necessary for the playing of any game of lawn tennis shall be fixed by, or under the direction of an officer of the Council duly appointed in that behalf.

(*c.*) A person shall not in the pleasure ground play or take part in any game of lawn tennis unless such person be wearing boots or shoes having soles of india-rubber or other material similarly adapted for preventing damage to the turf.

(*d.*) No game of lawn tennis shall be played or continue to be played on any day later than *a quarter of an hour* before the time fixed for closing the pleasure ground.

Special regulations as to *cricket.*

(7.) Every person resorting to any such space for the purpose of playing or taking part in any game of cricket shall observe and comply with the following conditions:—

(*a.*) Cricket shall not be played in the pleasure ground between the *thirtieth* day of *September* and the *first* day of *May*.

(*b.*) The wickets necessary for the playing of any game of cricket shall be pitched under the direction of an officer of the Council duly appointed in that behalf.

(*c.*) No game of cricket shall be played or continue to be played on any day later than *a quarter of an hour* before the time fixed for the closing of the pleasure ground.

Regulations as to *skating, sliding,* etc.

5.—(1.) A person shall not skate or slide in the pleasure ground except in such part of such ground as shall have been set apart by the Council for the purpose, and shall be indicated by a notice or notices affixed or set up in some conspicuous position in the pleasure ground, and at or near to each of the principal entrances thereto.

(2.) A person proceeding to or returning from, any ice in the pleasure ground shall not go or pass otherwise than by a path, road, or other usual means of access to the water, or by a path, track or other temporary means of access indicated by a notice or notices affixed or set up at or near to such path, track or means of access.

(3.) A person shall not go or remain upon any ice in the pleasure ground at any time when a notice or notices shall be affixed or set up in a conspicuous position on or over or near to such ice indicating that the ice is in a dangerous condition.

(4.) A person shall not go or attempt to go upon any ice in the pleasure ground at any time when a notice or notices shall be affixed or set up in a conspicuous position on, or over, or near to such ice, prohibiting any addition to the number of persons already occupying the same.

(5.) A person shall not throw, lay, place or deposit on any ice in the pleasure ground any chair, seat, stick, stone, gravel, sand, ashes, rubbish, or other article, substance or thing, or, not being an officer or servant of the Council, wilfully break or otherwise damage such ice, so as to interfere with the safe and convenient use of such ice by any person who may lawfully be or go thereon, or so as to render such ice unfit for use for the purpose of skating or sliding.

Regulations as to *fishing*.

6.—(1.) Subject as hereinafter provided, a person shall not take, injure or destroy, or attempt to take, injure, or destroy or wilfully disturb any fish in any lake, pond, stream, or other water in the pleasure ground.

Provided that this byelaw shall not be deemed to prohibit fishing in any such lake, pond, stream, or water, with a single rod and line, on the part of any person who shall previously have obtained from the Council, on application made to them, a ticket authorising such person to fish therein.

(2.) A person resorting to any lake, pond, stream, or other water in the pleasure ground for the purpose of fishing, shall not begin to fish at any time when the space available and allotted by the Council for the purpose is already occupied by such a number of persons fishing, and in such a manner as to render any addition to the number of such persons incompatible with the convenient use of such space by the persons already in occupation.

(3.) Every person resorting to any lake, pond, stream, or other water in the pleasure ground for the purpose of fishing, shall, in making preparation for and in fishing therein, use reasonable and proper care to avoid unduly interfering with the reasonable and proper use of the space available and allotted by the Council for the purpose by any other person engaged in making preparation for fishing or in fishing therein, or thereafter resorting to such space for the purpose of fishing.

(4.) A person shall not in any part of the pleasure ground, wilfully disturb, interrupt or annoy any person who may lawfully be making preparation for fishing, or fishing in any lake, pond, stream, or other water in the pleasure ground.

For regulating the number of persons to be carried in any pleasure boats on any lake or piece of water in the pleasure ground, the boat-houses and mooring-places for the same, and for fixing rates of hire and the qualifications of boatmen, and for securing their good and orderly conduct while in charge of any boat.

Number of persons to be carried.

7. Where a person shall have been licensed by the Council to let for hire any pleasure boats on any lake or piece of water in the pleasure ground subject to the condition that the number of persons carried in any such boat shall not at any time exceed a number fixed by or in pursuance of the conditions of such licence, such person, or a boatman in charge of such boat, shall not suffer any person to embark in such boat, at any time when the number of persons who shall have already embarked therein is equal to, or in excess of, the number so fixed.

Regulations as to boat-houses and mooring places.

8.—(1.) A person shall not wilfully, carelessly, or negligently remove, displace, deface, or defile, or carelessly or negligently injure, or destroy, any part of any boat-house or mooring-place for any pleasure boat in the pleasure ground.

(2.) A person shall not deposit any soil, dust, filth, ashes, rubbish or refuse in or upon any part of any such boat-house or mooring-place.

(3.) A person, not being an officer of the Council, or a person, or a servant of a person licensed by the Council to let for hire any pleasure boat on any lake or piece of water in the pleasure ground, shall not, without reasonable excuse, go into any boat-house for any such pleasure boat, or remain therein, except for the purpose of embarking in or debarking from any such pleasure boat.

(4.) A person shall not, at any mooring-place for any pleasure boat in the pleasure ground, wilfully and improperly unfasten, or interfere with the fastening of any such boat.

9. [A person or a servant of a person who shall have been licensed by the Council to let for hire any pleasure boat on any lake or piece of water in the pleasure ground, or a boatman in charge of any such pleasure boat] [any officer of the Council duly authorised in that behalf] shall be entitled to demand and take, in respect of the hire of any such pleasure boat, such of the rates following as may be applicable to the circumstances of the case :— **Rates of hire.**

Rates for time.

For the hire of a pleasure boat constructed or intended or adapted to be used to carry *one person* :—

	s.	d.
For the first hour - - - - - - - -		
For every half-hour or part of a half-hour after the first hour - - - - - - - -		

For the hire of a pleasure boat constructed or intended or adapted to be used to carry more than one, but not more than *three persons* :—

	s.	d.
For the first hour - - - - - - - -		
For every half-hour or part of a half-hour after the first hour - - - - - - - -		

For the hire of a pleasure boat constructed or intended or adapted to be used to carry *four or more persons* :—

	s.	d.
For the first hour - - - - - - - -		
For every half-hour or part of a half-hour after the first hour - - - - - - - -		
For the services of a boatman :—		
For the first hour - - - - - -		
For every half-hour or part of a half-hour after the first hour - - - - - -		

Special rate.

For conveyance in a pleasure boat once round the lake in the pleasure ground:—

	s. d.
For each person, not including any boatman or other person in charge of such boat - - -	

Qualifications of boatmen.

10. A boatman, not being a competent person, shall not row, steer, or take charge of any pleasure boat when used or let for hire on any lake or piece of water in the pleasure ground.

Conduct of boatmen.

11.—(1.) A boatman in charge of any pleasure boat in the pleasure ground shall comply with every reasonable requirement of any person hiring or being conveyed, or seeking to hire or to be conveyed in such pleasure boat, and shall conduct himself in an orderly manner, and with civility and propriety towards every such person.

(2.) A boatman shall not take charge of any pleasure boat in the pleasure ground while he is in a state of intoxication.

(3.) A boatman in charge of any pleasure boat in the pleasure ground shall not suffer any drunken or disorderly person to embark therein for the purpose of being carried for hire on any lake or piece of water in the pleasure ground, and shall not suffer any person under the age of *fourteen years*, or any person who is obviously incompetent to manage the boat, so to embark therein unless such person is accompanied by a boatman or other person competent to manage the same.

Penalties.

Penalties.

12. Every person who shall offend against any of the foregoing byelaws shall be liable for every such offence to a penalty of *five pounds*.

Provided, nevertheless, that the justices or court before whom any complaint may be made or any proceedings may be taken in respect of any such offence may, if they think fit, adjudge the payment, as a penalty, of any sum less than the full amount of the penalty imposed by this byelaw.

For providing for the removal from the pleasure ground of any person infringing any of the foregoing byelaws, by any officer of the Council or constable.

13. Every person who shall infringe any of the foregoing byelaws numbered 3* to 6,* both inclusive, may be removed from the pleasure ground by any officer of the Council, or by any constable, in any one of the several cases hereinafter specified; that is to say,— **Removal of offenders.**

(1.) Where the infraction of the byelaw is committed within the view of such officer or constable, and the name and residence of the person infringing the byelaw are unknown to and cannot be readily ascertained by such officer or constable;

(2.) Where the infraction of the byelaw is committed within the view of such officer or constable, and, from the nature of such infraction, or from any other fact of which such officer or constable may have knowledge, or of which he may be credibly informed, there may be reasonable ground for belief that the continuance in the pleasure ground of the person infringing the byelaw may result in another infraction of a byelaw, or that the removal of such person from the pleasure ground is otherwise necessary as a security for the proper use and regulation thereof.

Removal of offenders.—The power to provide for the removal of offenders (s. 164 of the Public Health Act, 1875) does not appear to be applicable to offenders against byelaws made under s. 44 (2) of the Public Health Acts Amendment Act, 1890 (clauses 7—11 in the present series).

Repeal.†

14. From and after the date of the confirmation of these byelaws, the [byelaw numbered in the series of] byelaws with respect to the pleasure ground which were made by the on the day of in the year one thousand eight hundred and , and which were confirmed by the Local Government Board on the day of in the year one thousand eight hundred and , shall be repealed. **Repeal.**

* *Verify these numbers before the byelaws are formally adopted.*

† *Where this series is adopted in its entirety, there will probably be one or more previously existing byelaws to repeal. The present clause, therefore, should be completed and added to the series.*

VILLAGE GREENS AND PARISH RECREATION GROUNDS.

MEMORANDUM.

Authority for the Byelaws.

A Parish Council are empowered by section 8 (1) (*d*) of the Local Government Act, 1894 (56 & 57 Vict. c. 73), "to make byelaws with respect to any recreation ground, village green, open space, or public walk, which is for the time being under their control, or to the expense of which they have contributed." The byelaws require confirmation by the Local Government Board; and the Board will probably call upon the Parish Council to show that any village green or recreation ground which the proposed clauses are intended to regulate, is one which comes within the terms of the section,—that is to say, that it is legally under their control; or that they have *bonâ fide* "contributed to the expense."

Local Authorities competent to make Byelaws.

The byelaws may be adopted by a Parish Council, by a Rural District Council, having the powers of a Parish Council under section 36 (4) of the Local Government Act, 1894, or by a Parish Meeting or an Urban District Council invested, in manner prescribed by the Act referred to, with the powers of a Parish Council in the matter (see sections 19 (10) and 33 (1)).

Scope of the Model Byelaws.

As the present series of byelaws is intended to apply only to a village green, or to a recreation ground provided under the Inclosure Acts, no mention is made of the matters dealt with in section 12 of the Inclosure Act, 1857 (20 & 21 Vict. c. 31). That enactment provides as regards any "town green," or "village green," or "land allotted and awarded upon any inclosure under the [Inclosure] Acts as a place for exercise and recreation," as follows,—

". . . If any person wilfully cause any injury or damage to any fence of any such town or village green or land, or wilfully and without lawful authority lead or drive any cattle or animal thereon, or wilfully lay any manure, soil, ashes, or rubbish, or other matter or thing thereon, or do any other act whatsoever to the injury of such town or village green or land, or to the interruption of the use or enjoyment thereof as a place for exercise and recreation, such person shall for every such offence, upon a summary conviction thereof before two justices . . . forfeit and pay, in any of the cases aforesaid, and for each and every such offence, over and above the damages occasioned thereby, any sum not exceeding forty shillings."

By operation of section 29 of the Commons Act, 1876 (39 & 40 Vict. c. 56), information with a view to such conviction may be given by "any inhabitant" of the parish within which the town or village green or recreation ground is situate, as well as by certain persons mentioned in section 12 of the Inclosure Act, 1857. The last-mentioned section also contains provisions with regard to the appropriation of any manure, etc., that may, in contravention of the enactment, be deposited upon the green or land, and with regard to the recovery of the penalty, the amount of the damage, and the expenses incurred in the removal of any such manure, etc., from the green. In view of these enactments a byelaw on any of the matters referred to would be unnecessary. Moreover, it may be regarded as a settled rule, that a byelaw enforceable by penalties should not extend to any matter which is punishable under the general law; and this also explains the omission from the series of any byelaws referring to other matters such as wilful acts of damage, etc. If, in any case, the Parish Council were desirous of regulating by means of byelaws any recreation ground, open space, or public walk, which was for the time being under their control, or to the expense of which they had contributed, but which was neither a village green nor a recreation ground provided under the Inclosure Acts, the present series could readily be adapted for the purpose.

Charges for the use of the village green or recreation ground.

Section 8 (1) (*d*) of the Local Government Act, 1894, makes applicable to the case of any village green or parish recreation ground which is within the scope of the enactment, the provisions of section 44 of the Public Health Acts Amendment Act, 1890 (53 & 54 Vict. c. 59). The latter section provides for the closing of a pleasure ground or any part thereof to the public, on such days as the Local Authority think fit, "not exceeding twelve days in any one year, nor four consecutive days on any one occasion," and not being Sunday or any public holiday. It enables the Local Authority, on any day when the ground is so closed, to "grant the use of the same, *either gratuitously or for payment*, to any public charity or institution, or for any agricultural, horticultural, or other show, or any other public purpose," or to themselves "use the same for any such show or purpose"; and the section further enacts that "the admission to the . . . . pleasure ground, or such part thereof, on the days when the same shall be so closed to the public, may be *either with or without payment* as directed by the . . . authority, or, with the consent of the . . . . authority, by the society or persons to whom the use of the . . . pleasure ground, or such part thereof, may be granted." Independently of this provision there is no power enabling the Parish Council to make any charge for the use of the village green or recreation ground, and the byelaws which they can make under section 8 (1) (*d*) of the Local Government Act, 1894, cannot fix any such charges.

Adoption of the Byelaws by the Parish Council.

The byelaws, after having received the preliminary approval of the Local Government Board,—for the purpose of obtaining which a draft of the proposed byelaws should, in the first instance, be submitted to that Board, in one of the draft forms issued by the publishers of the present work,—should be signed and sealed in the manner described in the note at the end of the series.

Other preliminaries to confirmation of the Byelaws.

Before the Local Government Board are applied to for formal confirmation of the byelaws, it will be necessary for the Parish Council to comply with certain other requirements, as to which the Council may expect in the ordinary course to receive full instructions from the Local Government Board, and these instructions should be carefully observed, with a view to the avoidance of subsequent expense and delay.

What is a "village green."—The expression "village green" has never been the subject of exact legal definition. It is, in general, an uninclosed space in or near a village, and open to common use. A parish or township not being a body corporate, such uninclosed space cannot be regarded as vested in the public. It is generally found that the soil is vested either in the lord of the manor in which the village lies, or in some private owner, and the right to keep the land uninclosed rests on the rights of such inhabitants as have by their tenements a right of common over the land, or on a reasonable local custom to use the land for recreation. The custom to use the land as a village green must be proved to have existed from time immemorial. A long unbroken exercise of it as of right must be shown (*Abbot* v. *Weekly* (1665), 1 Lev. 176). The right must be local, that is, confined to the inhabitants and not exercised by the world at large. Thus a custom for all the inhabitants of a parish to play at all kinds of lawful games, sports, and pastimes, in the close of A. at all reasonable times of the year, at their free will and pleasure, is good ; but a similar custom for all persons for the time being in the parish is bad (*Fitch* v. *Rawling* (1795), 2 H. Bl. 393 ; 3 R. R. 425. See also *Hammerton* v. *Honey* (1876), 24 W. R. 603 ; *Lancashire* v. *Hunt*, *Lancashire* v. *Maynard and Hunt* (1894), 10 T. L. R. 310, 448 ; 11 T. L. R. 49). A custom for the inhabitants of adjoining parishes to enter upon land in one of such parishes and enjoy recreation is also bad (*Edwards* v. *Jenkins*, [1896] 1 Ch. 308 ; 60 J. P. 167 ; 65 L. J. Ch. 222 ; 73 L. T. 574 ; 44 W. R. 407). A custom for the inhabitants of a parish to erect a maypole on the ground of a landowner within the parish, and dance round and about it, and otherwise enjoy any lawful and innocent recreation at any time in the year on the ground is reasonable and lawful (*Hall* v. *Nottingham* (1875), 1 Ex. D. 1 ; 45 L. J. Ex. 50 ; 33 L. T. 697 ; 24 W. R. 58), but when the right of the public to use is only occasional or intermittent, the land would not come within the designation of a village green.

VILLAGE GREENS AND PARISH RECREATION GROUNDS.

BYELAWS

MADE BY THE PARISH COUNCIL OF THE PARISH OF , WITH RESPECT TO THE [VILLAGE GREEN]* OF THE SAID PARISH.

Interpretation.

1. Throughout these byelaws the following words and expressions shall have the meanings hereinafter respectively assigned to them, that is to say,—

"Parish Council" means the Parish Council of the parish of ;

["Village Green"] means the [village green] of the said parish, situate at and commonly known as .

Protection of notice boards, etc.

2. A person shall not wilfully or improperly remove or displace or carelessly or negligently injure or destroy any board, plate, or tablet, or any support, fastening, or fitting of any board, plate, or tablet used or intended to be used for the exhibition of any byelaw or notice, and fixed or set up by the Parish Council on any part of the [village green], or in or on any building or structure thereon.

Protection of buildings, seats, etc.

3. A person shall not wilfully, carelessly or negligently remove, or carelessly or negligently deface, injure, or destroy any part of any building, or of any fixed or movable seat, or post, or of any other structure or erection on the [village green].

Vehicles.

4. A person shall not place, drive, or wheel, or cause or suffer to be placed, driven, or wheeled, on any part of the [village green] other than any road or cartway on or across the same, any cart, caravan, barrow, truck, or machine, or any

---

* *If the byelaws are to apply to a recreation ground, strike out the words "Village Green," and substitute "Recreation Ground," throughout the series.*

vehicle other than a wheeled chair drawn or propelled by hand, or a perambulator, chaise, mail cart, or other vehicle drawn or propelled by hand and used solely for the conveyance of a child or children, or an invalid.

Provided that the foregoing prohibition shall not apply in any case where, upon an application to the Parish Council to permit the placing on the [village green] of any cart, caravan, barrow, truck, machine, or vehicle, upon such occasion, or on such days as may be specified in such application, the Parish Council may grant, subject to such conditions as they may prescribe, permission to place such cart, caravan, barrow, truck, machine, or vehicle on such part of the [village green] as may be indicated by the Parish Council in granting such permission.

5. A person, other than a person acting under the authority of the Parish Council, shall not affix or post any bill, placard, or notice to or upon any tree, or to or upon any part of any building, or of any fixed or movable seat, or post, or of any other structure or erection on the [village green]. **Bill-posting.**

6. A person, other than a person acting under the authority of the Parish Council, shall not at any time take, dig, cut or remove any gravel, sand, sod, clay, turf, soil, or other similar substance in, on, or from the [village green]. **Taking gravel, turf, etc.**

Removal of gravel.—This byelaw would not confer upon the parish council themselves any power to remove gravel, etc., which they did not already possess.

7. A person shall not carelessly or negligently injure or destroy any timber, wood, brushwood, gorse, heather, or furze on the [village green]. **Protection of timber, etc.**

8. A person shall not wilfully, carelessly, or negligently commit any nuisance by soiling or defiling any part of any building, or of any fixed or movable seat, or post, or of any other structure or erection on the [village green]. **Nuisances.**

9. A person shall not throw or discharge on the [village green] any stone or other missile to the damage or danger of any person. **Throwing stones.**

10. A person shall not climb any tree or any post on the [village green]. **Climbing**

Protection of birds and birds' nests.

11. A person shall not, on the [village green], wilfully displace, disturb, injure or destroy any bird's nest, or wilfully take, injure, or destroy any bird's egg, or take, injure, or destroy any bird, or spread or use any net, or set or use any snare or other instrument or means for the taking, injury, or destruction of any bird.

Making fires

12. A person shall not light any fire on the [village green], or burn or do any act which might cause any timber, wood, brushwood, gorse, heather, furze, fern, earth, paper, rubbish, or other substance to take fire or be burned on the [village green].

Playing of games.

13. Every person resorting to the [village green] for the purpose of playing or taking part in any game of football, quoits, bowls, hockey, cricket, golf, or any other game which, by reason of the rules or manner of playing, or for the prevention of damage, danger, or discomfort to any person on the [village green] may necessitate, at any time during the continuance of the game, the exclusive use by the player or players of any space on the [green] shall comply with the following regulations :—

(1.) He shall, in making preparations for the playing of such game, and in the manner of playing, use reasonable and proper care to prevent undue interference with the reasonable and proper use of any space by any other person engaged in making preparation for playing, or in playing therein, or thereafter resorting to such space for the purpose of making preparation for playing or of playing therein :

(2.) He shall not at any time in any part of a space which is already occupied by other players begin to play without the permission of such other players :

(3.) Except in any case where the exclusive use of any space may have been granted by the Parish Council for the playing of any match, of which the occasion and character shall be such as to render expedient an extension of the time hereinafter specified, a player or company of players shall not, in making preparation for playing and in playing any game, use any part of such space for a longer time than *two hours* continuously, if, at the expiration of that time, any other player or company of players, for whose use no other part of the [village green] may be available, shall make known to such first-mentioned player or company of players an intention to use, for the purpose of playing, such space as shall have been previously used by such player or company of players.

14. A person shall not erect or place on the [village green] any post, rail, fence, pole, tent, booth, stand, swing, building, or other structure: Erecting tents, etc.

Provided that this prohibition shall not apply in any case where, upon an application to the Parish Council to permit the erection or placing on the [village green] of any post, rail, fence, pole, tent, booth, stand, swing, building, or other structure, upon such occasion or on such days as may be specified in such application, the Parish Council may grant, subject to such conditions as they may prescribe, permission to erect or place such post, rail, fence, pole, tent, booth, stand, swing, building, or other structure on such part of the [village green] as may be indicated by the Parish Council in granting such permission.

15. A person shall not, on any part of the [village green] beat, shake, sweep, brush, or cleanse any carpet, drugget, rug, or mat, or any other fabric retaining dust or dirt. Beating carpets.

16. A person shall not, on any part of the [village green] or any tree, bush, post, rail, fence, pole, building or structure thereon, hang, spread, or deposit any linen or other fabric for the purpose of drying or bleaching. Drying and bleaching clothes.

17. A person shall not frequent or use the [village green] for the purpose of betting or wagering or of agreeing to make any bet or wager. Betting, etc.

18. A person shall not on the [village green] use any indecent or obscene language to the annoyance of any other person using the [village green]. Bad language.

19. A person shall not wilfully obstruct, disturb, interrupt, or annoy any other person in the proper use of the [village green], or any officer of the Parish Council in the proper execution of his duty. Disturbance, interruption, and annoyance.

Penalties.

Penalties.

20. Every person who shall offend against any of the foregoing byelaws shall be liable for every such offence to a penalty of *five pounds*.

Provided, nevertheless, that the justices or court before whom any complaint may be made or any proceedings may be taken in respect of any such offence may, if they think fit, adjudge the payment, as a penalty, of any sum less than the full amount of the penalty imposed by this byelaw.

Removal of offenders.

Removal of offenders.

21. Every person who shall infringe any byelaw for the regulation of the [village green] may be removed therefrom by any officer of the Parish Council, or by any constable, in any one of the several cases hereinafter specified; that is to say,—

(1.) Where the infraction of the byelaw is committed within the view of such officer or constable, and the name and residence of the person infringing the byelaw are unknown to and cannot be readily ascertained by such officer or constable:

(2.) Where the infraction of the byelaw is committed within the view of such officer or constable, and, from the nature of such infraction, or from any other fact of which such officer or constable may have knowledge, or of which he may be credibly informed, there may be reasonable ground for belief that the continuance on the [village green] of the person infringing the byelaw may result in another infraction of a byelaw, or that the removal of such person from the [village green] is otherwise necessary as a security for the proper use and regulation thereof.

Saving.

Saving.

* **22.** Nothing in, or done under any of the foregoing byelaws shall affect any right, power, or privilege lawfully exerciseable by any person in, or over, or in respect of the [village green].

Adoption of the byelaws.—Section 3 (9) of the Local Government Act, 1894, taken in connection with s. 182 of the Public Health Act, 1875, requires

* *This byelaw may be omitted if not required.*

that the byelaws shall be signed at a meeting of the Parish Council by the chairman presiding, and two other members of the Council, and that each of the persons signing should affix his seal. A wafer seal, or any other kind of seal that may be convenient, may be adopted for the purpose. But there should be a separate seal in connection with each signature, and there should be no reference to any seal as the seal of the Parish Council. The Council, as a body, are not entitled to use a seal. The following form is suggested :—

GIVEN under our hands and seals at a meeting of the Parish Council held after due notice thereof this day of , 18 .

(L.S.)
Presiding Chairman at the said Meeting.

(L.S.)
(L.S.)
Two members of the Parish Council.

WHIRLIGIGS, SWINGS, SHOOTING GALLERIES, ETC.

MEMORANDUM.

Authority for making Byelaws.

Section 38 of the Public Health Acts Amendment Act, 1890 (53 & 54 Vict. c. 59), provides that "an urban authority may make byelaws for the prevention of danger from whirligigs and swings when such whirligigs and swings are driven by steam power, and from the use of firearms in shooting ranges and galleries."

Scope of the Model Byelaws.

The Act above-mentioned contains no definition of the terms "whirligig," "swing," "shooting range" and "shooting gallery"; and the byelaws cannot define those terms. It will be a question for the decision, in the first instance, of the justices before whom any proceedings may be taken for the enforcement of any byelaws such as those contained in the model series annexed, whether, in any particular case, the erection or thing to which such proceedings relate is one to which the terms of the section are applicable. It will, however, be observed that byelaws are authorised with regard only to whirligigs and swings "driven by steam power"; and as regards shooting ranges, it is to be inferred from the use of the expression "*in* shooting ranges" that a certain class of such ranges only can be dealt with. The byelaws can, in any case, only extend to "the prevention of danger." Structural matters, therefore, can be dealt with only in so far as may be necessary for this purpose.

Local Authorities competent to make Byelaws.

The model byelaws annexed can be adopted by any Urban District Council, after the adoption by them of Part III. of the Public Health Acts Amendment Act, 1890; and by any Rural

District Council as regards any portion of their district in which, by an order of the Local Government Board, section 38 of the Act has been put in force. (See ss. 3 and 5 of the Act.)

Confirmation of the Byelaws.

The byelaws made by any Local Authority under section 38 of the Act above-mentioned require confirmation by the Local Government Board, and in compliance with the rule adopted by that Board, any proposed byelaws of the kind should be submitted to them, in the first instance, in draft. Draft forms for this purpose are issued by the publishers of the present work.

WHIRLIGIGS, SWINGS, SHOOTING GALLERIES, ETC.

BYELAWS

MADE BY THE* WITH RESPECT TO WHIRLIGIGS, SWINGS, AND SHOOTING RANGES AND GALLERIES IN THE† .

Interpretation of terms.

Interpretation.

1. Throughout these byelaws, the following words and expressions shall have the meanings hereinafter respectively assigned to them, that is to say,—

"The Council" means the* ;

"The District" means the† ;

"Whirligig" and "swing" respectively mean a whirligig and a swing which is driven by steam power, and is erected, fixed, or set up within the district, and used or let, or intended to be used or let for hire ;

"Shooting range or gallery" means a shooting range or gallery within the district, to which the public are admitted, with or without payment, and in which firearms are used or let out for hire.

"Proprietor," when used in relation to a whirligig or swing, or a shooting range or gallery, includes any person who, either on his own behalf, or on behalf of any other person, lets to hire, or causes or suffers to be used or let for hire, such whirligig or swing, or such shooting range or gallery, or any seat or place in or upon such whirligig or swing, or any firearms in such shooting range or gallery.

---

* "Mayor, aldermen, and burgesses of the borough of , acting by the Council"; *or,* "Urban [*or* Rural] District Council of ," *as the case may be.*

† *Insert name of borough or urban or rural district, or if the byelaws are to apply to part only of a rural district* "that portion of the rural district of which comprises the contributory places of ," *as the case may be.*

For the prevention of danger from whirligigs and swings when such whirligigs and swings are driven by steam power.

2. Every proprietor of a whirligig or swing shall, for the prevention of danger from such whirligig or swing,— Duties of proprietor.

(1.) cause such whirligig or swing to be so placed as to have about it a clear space, the distance across which, measured upon the ground from the outermost point covered by such whirligig or swing, or which such whirligig or swing may overhang, shall in every part be equal at least to the greatest height of such whirligig or swing;

(2.) cause such whirligig or swing to be erected in a proper manner, and every part thereof to be carefully and securely fixed;

(3.) cause every part of such whirligig or swing and of the apparatus for driving the same to be maintained at all times in good repair and condition, and to be under proper management and control;

(4.) cause the apparatus for driving such whirligig or swing to be tended and regulated by a competent person responsible exclusively for the care and management of such apparatus;

(5.) cause such whirligig or swing, if in motion, and if any person riding in, or upon such whirligig or swing be ill, or be desirous of alighting therefrom, to be stopped as quickly as may be practicable, for the purpose of allowing such person to alight, or to be removed from such whirligig or swing.

3.—(1.) The proprietor or any other person for the time being having the management or control of a whirligig or swing, or of the apparatus for driving the same, or of any part of such whirligig or swing, or of such apparatus shall, in the exercise of such management or control, take all reasonable and proper care so as to prevent danger from such whirligig or swing. Duties of person in charge.

(2.) He shall not cause or suffer such whirligig or swing to be driven at any greater speed than shall be consistent with safety, having regard to the age and sex of any persons riding in or upon such whirligig or swing, and to all other circumstances attending or affecting the use of such whirligig or swing.

(3.) He shall not cause or suffer any person to enter or mount upon such whirligig or swing at any time when such whirligig or swing shall be already occupied by the full number of persons for whose accommodation such whirligig or swing shall be constructed or intended or adapted to be used.

Duties of other persons.

4. A person shall not—

(1.) knowingly enter or mount upon, or seek to enter or mount upon any whirligig or swing, or any part thereof, at any time when such whirligig or swing, or such part thereof, shall be already occupied by the full number of persons for whose accommodation such whirligig or swing shall be constructed, or intended, or adapted to be used:

(2.) be guilty of any disorderly or improper conduct so that the use of such whirligig or swing may be attended with danger to any person:

(3.) wilfully and improperly, or carelessly or negligently interfere with the due management and control of such whirligig or swing, or with the apparatus for driving the same, or with any fastening, fitting, or appliance connected with such whirligig or swing, or with such apparatus; or

(4.) otherwise do any act which may cause danger from such whirligig or swing.

For the prevention of danger from the use of fireams in shooting ranges and galleries.

Duties of proprietor.

5. The proprietor of a shooting range or gallery shall, for the prevention of danger from the use of firearms in such shooting range or gallery,—

(1.) cause the several parts of such shooting range or gallery to be properly put together and securely fixed:

(2.) cause every part of such shooting range or gallery, within, along, or towards which it may be intended that any firearm shall be discharged, to be constructed of iron of such strength and thickness as shall be sufficient to resist any missile or projectile that may be discharged from such firearm:

(3.) cause the mode of construction of such shooting range or gallery to be such that no missile or projectile that may be discharged from any firearm used therein can escape from such shooting range or gallery, if such firearm, at the moment of discharge, be pointed, as required by the byelaws in that behalf,* towards any target or mark that may be within such shooting range or gallery:

(4.) cause every part of such shooting range or gallery within, along, or towards which it may be intended that any firearm shall be discharged, to be maintained at all times in good repair and condition:

(5.) cause such shooting range or gallery, at all times when the public are admitted thereto, to be under the management and control of a sufficient number of competent persons:

(6.) cause the letting to hire and use by any person of any firearm in such shooting range or gallery to be under the management and control of a competent person directly responsible therefor.

6.—(1.) The proprietor or any other person for the time being having the management or control of a shooting range or gallery, or of any part thereof, shall, in the exercise of such management or control, take all reasonable and proper care so as to prevent danger from the use of firearms in such shooting range or gallery. **Duties of persons in charge.**

(2.) Every person having in pursuance of the byelaw in that behalf,† the management and control of the letting to hire and use by any person of any firearm in a shooting range or gallery, shall not at any time cause or suffer to be used in such firearm any greater charge than is consistent with safety; and shall cause every such firearm, when loaded or being loaded, to be pointed towards any target or mark that may be within such shooting range or gallery; and shall not suffer any loaded firearm to be taken out of such shooting range or gallery.

7.—(1.) Notwithstanding anything in the foregoing byelaw, a person hiring or using any firearm in a shooting range or gallery, shall not, while such firearm is loaded or being loaded, **Duties of other persons.**

* See clauses 6 (2) and 7 (1), *post*.

† See clause 5 (6), *supra*.

cause such firearm to be pointed otherwise than towards any target or mark that may be within such shooting range or gallery, and shall not take any loaded firearm out of such shooting range or gallery.

(2.) A person shall not in a shooting range or gallery be guilty of any disorderly or improper conduct, so as to cause danger in connection with the use of any firearm in such shooting range or gallery.

(3.) A person shall not wilfully and improperly or carelessly or negligently interfere with the due management and control of the letting to hire and use by any person of any firearm in a shooting range or gallery, or with any shield, fastening or fitting in or forming part of such shooting range or gallery, and intended to secure or contribute to the safe use of firearms therein.

Penalties.

Penalties. **8.** Every person who shall offend against any of the foregoing byelaws shall be liable for every such offence to a penalty of *five pounds*, and in the case of a continuing offence to a further penalty of *forty shillings* for each day after written notice of the offence from the Council:

Provided nevertheless, that the justices or court before whom any complaint may be made or any proceedings may be taken in respect of any such offence may, if they think fit, adjudge the payment, as a penalty, of any sum less than the full amount of the penalty imposed by this byelaw.

PART VI.

SCAVENGING.

REMOVAL OF FILTH THROUGH THE STREETS.

MEMORANDUM.

Authority for the Byelaws.

Byelaws on this subject may be made under sub-section (1) of section 26 of the Public Health Acts Amendment Act, 1890 (53 & 54 Vict. c. 59), or any local Act containing similar provisions. The sub-section referred to enacts as follows :—

"An urban authority may make byelaws in respect of the following matters, namely :—

"(*a*.) For prescribing the times for the removal or carriage through the streets of any fœcal or offensive or noxious matter or liquid, whether such matter or liquid shall be in course of removal or carriage from within or without or through their district:

"(*b*.) For providing that the vessel, receptacle, cart, or carriage used therefor shall be properly constructed and covered so as to prevent the escape of any such matter or liquid :

"(*c*.) For compelling the cleansing of any place whereon such matter or liquid shall have been dropped or spilt in such removal or carriage."

Local Authorities competent to make Byelaws.

Byelaws under the enactment above-cited can only be made by an Urban District Council after the adoption by them in manner required by the Act (see section 3), of Part III. of the Public Health Acts Amendment Act, 1890, and by a Rural District Council after the provisions of section 26 (1) have been put in force in their district, or some part thereof, by an order of the Local Government Board (section 5).

Scope of the Model Byelaws.

The byelaws may regulate the carriage through the streets of the district to which they apply, of filth which is brought into or through the district from an adjoining or neighbouring district, as well as filth collected and removed from premises within the first-mentioned district. A series of this kind, therefore, will be found very useful in diminishing the nuisance often experienced (*e.g.*), in urban districts on the outskirts of a large town, in connection with the removal into the country of night-soil and other offensive matter from the town.

Exemption of stable manure.

It is not usually considered necessary to bring the removal of stable manure within the scope of such byelaws as may be made under paragraph (*a*) or (*b*) of section 26 (1) of the Act above-mentioned, and attention may be drawn to the terms of the model clauses 2 and 3, which exempt this work from the operation of those particular clauses.

Hours for removal of filth.

The Local Government Board lay great stress on the performance of all scavenging operations by daylight. The hours prescribed by one of that Board's supplementary model clauses (No. 4a of the series as to nuisances*), for emptying or cleansing of privies, cesspools, and other receptacles for filth, are from six to half-past past eight o'clock in the morning from the 1st March to the end of October, and from seven to half-past nine o'clock in the morning from the 1st November to the end of February. The cartage of other offensive matters, however, might be permitted to commence half-an-hour, or even an hour earlier each day, assuming that the requirements of clauses 3 and 4 of the present series are duly enforced.

Confirmation of the Byelaws.

Byelaws under section 26 (1) of the Public Health Acts Amendment Act, 1890, require confirmation by the Local Government Board. They should be submitted to that Board, in the first instance, in draft.

---

* See Model Byelaws, vol. i., pp. 34, 35.

REMOVAL OF FILTH THROUGH STREETS.

BYELAWS

MADE BY THE* WITH RESPECT TO THE REMOVAL OR CARRIAGE THROUGH THE STREETS OF FŒCAL OR OFFENSIVE OR NOXIOUS MATTER OR LIQUID WITHIN THE† .

Interpretation of terms.

1. Throughout these byelaws, the following words and expressions shall have the meanings hereinafter respectively assigned to them, that is to say,— **Interpretation.**

"Council" means the* ;

"District" means the†

For prescribing the times for the removal or carriage through the streets of any fœcal or offensive or noxious matter or liquid, whether such matter or liquid shall be in course of removal from within or without or through the district.

2. A person shall not, within the district, remove or carry, or cause to be removed or carried, through the streets, any fœcal or offensive or noxious matter or liquid, other than stable manure, whether such matter or liquid shall be in course of removal or carriage from within or without or through the dirtrict, except between and o'clock‡ in the morning from the *first* day of *March* to the *thirty-first* day of *October* (both inclusive), and between and o'clock in the morning during the rest of the year. **Hours for removal of filth.**

---

* "Mayor, aldermen, and burgesses of the borough of , acting by the Council"; *or,* "Urban [*or* Rural] District Council of ," *as the case may be.*

† *Insert name of borough or urban or rural district or, if the byelaws are to apply to part only of a rural district,* "that portion of the Rural District of which comprises the contributory places of ," *as the case may be.*

‡ *As to the hours, see previous page.*

For providing that the vessel, receptacle, cart or carriage used for such removal or carriage through the streets shall be properly constructed and covered so as to prevent the escape of any such matter or liquid.

Construction of carts, etc.

3. A person who, within the district, shall remove or carry, or cause to be removed or carried through the streets, any fœcal or offensive or noxious matter or liquid other than stable manure, whether such matter or liquid shall be in course of removal or carriage from within or without or through the district, shall not, for the purposes of such removal or carriage, use or cause to be used any vessel, receptacle, cart or carriage, which is not properly constructed and covered so as to prevent the escape of any such matter or liquid.

For compelling the cleansing of any place whereon such matter or liquid shall have been dropped or spilt in such removal or carriage.

Cleansing of streets if filth dropped or spilt.

4. Every person who, in the removal or carriage through the streets of any fœcal or offensive or noxious matter or liquid, whether such matter or liquid shall be in course of removal or carriage from within or without or through the district, shall cause or suffer any such matter or liquid to be dropped or spilt on any footway, pavement, or carriageway, shall forthwith cause the place whereon such matter or liquid shall have been dropped or spilt to be thoroughly cleansed.

Penalties.

Penalties.

5. Every person who shall offend against any of the foregoing byelaws shall be liable for every such offence to a penalty of *five pounds.*

Provided nevertheless, that the justices or court before whom any complaint may be made or any proceedings may be taken in respect of any such offence, may, if they think fit, adjudge the payment, as a penalty, of any sum less than the full amount of the penalty imposed by this byelaw.

REMOVAL OF HOUSE REFUSE.

MEMORANDUM,

Authority for making the Byelaws.

Section 26 (2) of the Public Health Acts Amendment Act, 1890 (53 & 54 Vict. c. 59), provides that,—

" Where a local authority themselves undertake or contract for the removal of house refuse they may make byelaws imposing on the occupier of any premises duties in connection with such removal so as to facilitate the work which the local authority undertake or contract for."

Local Authorities competent to make Byelaws.

Byelaws may be made under this enactment by any Urban or Rural District Council who, under section 42 of the Public Health Act, 1875 (38 & 39 Vict. c. 55), undertake or contract for the removal of house refuse from premises, if Part III. of the Act of 1890 has been adopted by the Council in manner provided by section 3, or (in the case of a Rural District Council) if they have been invested with the necessary powers by an order of the Local Government Board under section 5 of the latter Act.

A Local Authority so undertaking or contracting are precluded from making byelaws with regard to the removal of house refuse under section 44 of the Act of 1875; and if the Local Authority are making, or have made, byelaws under that section with respect to nuisances, and such byelaws prohibit the deposit of dust, ashes, and rubbish on the footways, the adoption of the present series will make it desirable to amend the nuisance byelaws, so as to provide that the prohibition shall not apply to the deposit on the kerbstone, or outer edge of any footway of house refuse intended for removal by or on behalf of the District Council, if contained in properly constructed receptacles.*

---

* See Model Byelaws, vol. i., p. 34.

Confirmation of the Byelaws.

The byelaws suggested in the accompanying series require confirmation by the Local Government Board. They should be submitted to that Board, in the first instance, in draft. Draft forms for the purpose are supplied by the publishers of this work.

House refuse.—There is no definition in the Public Health Acts of what constitutes house refuse. In *London and Provincial Laundry Co.* v. *Willesden Local Board* (*infra*), CHARLES, J., thought that "the expression 'house refuse' is used to cover what Lord BRAMWELL in *Lyndon* v. *Standbridge* (*infra*) calls 'house occupation, inhabitancy or domestic rubbish.'" In *Lyndon* v. *Standbridge* (1857), 26 L. J. Ex. 386, it was held that, under the Towns Improvement Clauses Act, 1847 (10 & 11 Vict. c. 34), house refuse does not extend to dust and ashes the exclusive produce of manufactories; and in *London and Provincial Steam Laundry Co.* v. *Willesden Local Board*, [1892] 2 Q. B. 271; 67 L. T. 499; 40 W. R. 557; 56 J. P. 696, it was held that under the Public Health Act, 1875, it does not include clinkers from the boilers of a steam laundry. The decisions under the Metropolis Management Act, 1855 (18 & 19 Vict. c. 120), may be of some use in this connection. In *St. Martin's Vestry* v. *Gordon*, [1891] 1 Q. B. 61; 60 L. J. M. C. 37; 64 L. T. 243; 39 W. R. 295; 55 J. P. 437; 7 T. L. R. 71, it was held that clinkers produced in the furnaces of boilers belonging to an hotel, used to generate steam for the purpose of supplying power for electric lighting and for warming and cooking and other purposes of the hotel, are not refuse of a trade, manufacture, or business within the meaning of s. 128 of the Metropolis Management Act, 1855, and therefore the scavengers, under s. 125 of the Act, are bound to remove them without payment. In *Holborn Union (Guardians of)* v. *St. Leonard's, Shoreditch* (1876), 2 Q. B. D. 145; 46 L. J. Q. B. 843; 27 W. R. 504; 43 J. P. 367, it was held that a metropolitan vestry was bound to remove the dirt, ashes, rubbish, and filth from a workhouse within their jurisdiction, even although the workhouse was under a local Act rated at a less amount than other property in the parish. In *Gay* v. *Cadby* (1877), 2 C. P. D. 391; 46 L. J. M. C. 260; 36 L. T. 410; 41 J. P. 503, it was held that ashes arising from coals burnt in the furnace of a steam engine used for the purpose of sawing and lifting timber and other materials, for carrying on the business of a pianoforte manufacturer, are refuse of a trade, business, or manufacture within the Metropolis Management Act, 1855, s. 128. It was held in *Collins* v. *Paddington Vestry* (1879), 48 L. J. Q. B. 345; 40 L. T. 843; 27 W. R. 504; 43 J. P. 367, that under the Metropolis Management Act, the duty of the vestry was to remove everything which might be injurious from a sanitary point of view. Accordingly, when the Paddington Vestry sold to the plaintiff "all the breeze, dust, cinders, ashes, dirt, offal, garbage, filth, and refuse which shall be collected and received by them within the parish of Paddington," to be collected by the vestry and delivered to the plaintiff, and during the collection the servants of the vestry appropriated various articles, called "tots," which had been thrown into the dustbin by the owners, in order to be got rid of, it was held in action under the contract for the value of the tots so appropriated that the plaintiff could not recover.

In *R.* v. *Bridge* (1890), 24 Q. B. D. 609; 59 L. J. M. C. 49; 62 L. T. 297; 38 W. R. 464; 54 J. P. 629, when a police magistrate, acting under the Metropolis Management Act, 1855, s. 129, decided that certain ashes from the furnaces of an hotel were not "refuse of trade," and declined to state a case on the ground that the decision was "final and conclusive," and no point of law arose; it was held that there was a question of law on the construction of s. 129, and that the magistrate was not entitled to refuse to state a case. The case was afterwards stated, and came before the court under the title of *St. Martin's Vestry* v. *Gordon*, *supra*.

REMOVAL OF HOUSE REFUSE.

BYELAWS

MADE BY THE* FOR IMPOSING ON THE OCCUPIER OF ANY PREMISES IN THE† DUTIES IN CONNECTION WITH THE REMOVAL OF HOUSE REFUSE, SO AS TO FACILITATE THE WORK OF REMOVAL.

Interpretation.

1. Throughout these byelaws the following words and expressions shall have the meanings hereinafter respectively assigned to them, that is to say,—

"Council" means the * ;

"District" means the † ;

"At the prescribed times" means on such days and at such hour of the day as may from time to time be fixed by the Council, and may be notified by advertisement in a newspaper, or otherwise by public announcement in the district;

"In the prescribed place" means, in relation to any premises, (*a*) on the kerbstone or outer edge of the footpath immediately in front of such premises, or (*b*) outside such premises in any street at the rear or side of such premises, not being the principal approach or means of access to any building, or (*c*) in a conveniently accessible position on such premises, according as the Council shall have prescribed by written notice served upon the occupier.

Ashbins to be placed outside premises, or elsewhere

2. The occupier of any premises within the district shall at the prescribed times and in the prescribed place, deposit one

* "Mayor, aldermen, and burgesses of the borough of , acting by the Council"; *or*, "Urban [*or* Rural] District Council of ," *as the case may be.*

† *Insert name of borough or urban or rural district or, if the byelaws are to apply to part only of a rural district*, "that portion of the Rural District of which comprises the contributory places of ," *as the case may be.*

or more moveable receptacles, each of a capacity not exceeding *six cubic feet*, in which shall be placed the house refuse which may have accumulated on such premises, and may be intended for removal by or on behalf of the Council. **as required by Council.**

Penalties.

3. Every person who shall offend against the foregoing byelaw shall be liable for every such offence to a penalty of *forty shillings*: **Penalties.**

Provided nevertheless that the justices or court before whom any complaint may be made, or any proceedings may be taken, in respect of any such offence may, if they think fit, adjudge the payment as a penalty of any sum less than the full amount of the penalty imposed by this byelaw.

PART VII.

PUBLIC CONVENIENCES AND CABMEN'S SHELTERS.

PUBLIC SANITARY CONVENIENCES.

MEMORANDUM.

Authority for the Byelaws and Regulations.

Byelaws and regulations such as those suggested in the annexed model series may be made under section 20 of the Public Health Acts Amendment Act, 1890 (53 & 54 Vict. c. 59), or under any local Act containing similar provisions. The enactment referred to, so far as it is material, is as follows :—

"20.—(1.) Where an urban authority provide and maintain for public accommodation any sanitary conveniences, such authority may—

"(i.) Make regulations with respect to the management thereof and make byelaws as to the decent conduct of persons using the same ;

"(ii.) Let the same from time to time for any term not exceeding three years at such rent and subject to such conditions as they may think fit ;

"(iii.) Charge such fees for the use of any waterclosets provided by them as they may think proper.

* * * * *

"(4.) Nothing in this section shall extend to any sanitary convenience now or hereafter to be erected by any railway company within their railway station yard or the approaches thereto."

The expression "sanitary convenience," as used in this enactment, includes urinals, waterclosets, earthclosets, privies, ashpits, and any similar convenience (section 11).

Scope of the Model Byelaws and Regulations.

It will be noticed that the byelaws authorised by the provisions of sub-section (1) (i.) of section 20 relate to the "decent conduct" of persons using the public sanitary conveniences.

It does not seem necessary to construe the term "decent conduct" in relation to the use of a public sanitary convenience as if it were merely the antithesis of "indecent conduct" in the sense in which that phrase would ordinarily be understood. Any act, which though not positively indecent, could be described as "not a decent act" on the part of a person using a convenience maintained at the cost, and for the use of the public, might, apparently, be prohibited by the byelaws, if not otherwise dealt with by law. The proviso to the model byelaw 7 is suggested in consequence of the provisions of the Indecent Advertisements Act, 1889 (52 & 53 Vict. c. 18); but the clause assumes that bill-sticking in, and the marking of walls of a public sanitary convenience are not "decent conduct," irrespective of the "decency" or otherwise of the contents of the bill, or of the writing or figure *per se*. The regulations which the statute authorises to be made "with respect to the management" of public sanitary conveniences are not enforceable by penalties. Hence, it is practically useless to prescribe regulations to be observed by the persons using the conveniences. The model series, therefore, is limited to matters as to which the attendant in charge can properly be made responsible. The continuance of his employment by the Local Authority will naturally be made dependent on the observance by him of these, and any other similar regulations which may be made by the authority.

Local Authorities competent to make Byelaws and Regulations.

The model series of byelaws and regulations can only be adopted where the Local Authority provide and maintain sanitary conveniences for public accommodation. A Rural District Council cannot do this unless invested by an order of the Local Government Board, with the powers of an Urban District Council under section 39 of the Public Health Act, 1875 (38 & 39 Vict. c. 55); and they can only make byelaws and regulations under section 20 of the Public Health Acts Amendment Act, 1890, if that section is put in force in their district, or in any part thereof in the same way (see section 5 of the Act of 1890). An Urban District Council obtain power to make byelaws and regulations by adopting Part III. of the Public Health Acts Amendment Act, 1890 (section 3).

Adoption of Byelaws and Regulations.

Both the byelaws and the regulations should be adopted under seal of the Local Authority, the sealing, in each case, being properly attested, and the actual date of sealing being inserted in the attestation.

Confirmation of the Byelaws.

The byelaws require confirmation by the Local Government Board, but not the regulations (see section 188 of the Public Health Act, 1875). The byelaws should be submitted to that Board, in the first instance, in draft.

Publication of the Regulations.

The Local Authority may cause any regulations made by them under section 20 (1) of the Public Health Acts Amendment Act, 1890, to be published in such manner as they think fit (section 188 of the Public Health Act, 1875).

Proper and convenient situation.—Where the Urban Authority provide the convenience under s. 39 of the Public Health Act, 1875, it is sometimes difficult to determine what is a proper and convenient situation. The matter is left to a large extent to the discretion of the Local Authority, and it has been laid down that their decision will not be interfered with by the courts in the absence of bad faith, or arbitrary, perverse and vexatious conduct on their part in the selection of a site, or positive evidence of the existence of a nuisance. Sir G. JESSELL, M.R., held that in the absence of improper motives, the Urban Authority had an absolute discretion in choosing the site (*Mason* v. *Wallasey Local Board* (1876), 58 J. P. 477; see also *Graham* v. *Newcastle-upon-Tyne Corporation* (1892), 67 L. T. 790; 2 R. 254). "It is the duty of the urban authority to take into consideration the propriety and convenience of the spot selected in this sense, viz., they must see that the place is one which requires the convenience, and then choose a site which is proper and convenient, both with reference to the public and with reference to the surrounding land, and the owners and occupiers of houses in the neighbourhood" (CHITTY, J., in *Pethick* v. *Mayor, etc., of Plymouth* (1894), 58 J. P. 476; 42 W. R. 246; 70 L. T. 304; 10 T. L. R. 204; 8 R. 107). Accordingly, where the plaintiff was the owner of numerous houses of a superior class abutting on a road overlooking a public park, and the Urban Authority resolved to erect a urinal and lavatory in the park about 230 feet from the plaintiff's nearest house and in full view of them all, and the plaintiff moved for an injunction to restrain the Urban Authority from erecting the proposed building so as to cause a nuisance to himself and his tenants and proved that the letting value of his houses would be diminished, and that there were other sites more convenient, but failed to prove that any nuisance by smell was likely to arise, the court refused an injunction (*Pethick* v. *Mayor, etc., of Plymouth, supra*; see also *Spicer* v. *Mayor, etc., of Margate* (1880), 24 Sol. J. 821).

Where a Local Board erected a public urinal partly upon a highway and partly upon a strip of land belonging to the plaintiff, and so near to other adjoining land of the plaintiff as to be a nuisance (as the learned judge found) to her and her tenants, and to depreciate the value of her property, DENMAN, J., granted a mandatory injunction to restrain the Board from continuing the urinal upon her land or so near thereto as to cause injury or annoyance to her or her tenants (*Sellors* v. *Matlock Bath Local Board* (1885), 14 Q. B. D. 928; 52 L. T. 762).

For decisions under the corresponding section (88) of the Metropolis Management Act, 1855 (17 & 18 Vict. c. 120), see *Biddulph* v. *Vestry of St. George, Hanover Square* (1863), 33 L. J. Ch. 411; 3 De G. J. & S. 493; 8 L. T. (N.S.) 558; 2 N. R. 212; and *Vernon* v. *Vestry of St. James', Westminster* (1879), 16 Ch. D. 449; 50 L. J. Ch. 81; 44 L. T. 229).

In *Tunbridge Wells* (*Corporation*) v. *Baird*, [1896] A. C. 434; 60 J. P. 788; 65 L. J. Q. B. 451; 74 L. T. 385; 12 T. L. R. 372; affirming Court of Appeal, [1894] 2 Q. B. 867; 59 J. P. 36; 71 L. T. 211, the question was raised whether the vesting of a street in a Local Authority under s. 149 of the Public Health Act, 1875, vests the soil below the surface so as to entitle them to construct an underground lavatory, and it was held that the Act did not vest the sub-soil of a street in the Local Authority, but conferred only so much property as was sufficient to enable it to enforce the control and management of such street, and the Local Authority had no power to construct such lavatory. In London, however, the subsoil of any road, exclusive of the footway adjoining any building or the curtilage of a building, is vested in the sanitary authority, for such purposes, by s. 44 (2) of the Public Health (London) Act, 1891 (54 & 55 Vict. c. 76).

CONDUCT OF PERSONS USING SANITARY CONVENIENCES.

BYELAWS

MADE BY THE* AS TO THE DECENT CONDUCT OF PERSONS USING THE SANITARY CONVENIENCES PROVIDED AND MAINTAINED FOR PUBLIC ACCOMMODATION BY THE SAID COUNCIL WITHIN THE † .

Interpretation of terms.

1. Throughout these byelaws the following words and expressions shall have the meanings hereinafter respectively assigned to them, that is to say,— Interpretation.

"Council" means the * ;

"Sanitary conveniences" means the several sanitary conveniences provided and maintained for public accommodation by the Council;

"Attendant" means the person for the time being appointed by the Council to take charge of any of the sanitary conveniences.

As to the decent conduct of persons using the sanitary conveniences.

2.‡ A person using the sanitary conveniences shall not enter any watercloset forming part of such conveniences, and not being a watercloset set apart by the Council for use without payment, unless he shall have first paid to the attendant the sum charged by the Council as a fee for the use of such watercloset. Entering watercloset without paying.

[**2.**‡ A person using the sanitary conveniences shall not enter any watercloset forming part of such conveniences, and

---

* "Mayor, aldermen, and burgesses of the borough of , acting by the Council"; *or*, "Urban [*or* Rural] District Council of ," *as the case may be.*

† *Insert name of borough or urban or rural district, or, if the byelaws are to apply to part only of a rural district,* "that portion of the Rural District of which comprises the contributory places of ," *as the case may be.*

‡ *These two clauses are suggested as alternatives.*

not being a watercloset set apart by the Council for use without payment, unless he shall have first placed in the box or receptacle provided for the purpose, and marked "For pennies only," the sum charged by the Council as a fee for the use of such watercloset.]

Entering waterclosets out of turn.

3. A person using the sanitary conveniences shall not, by forcible or improper means,—

(1.) enter, or seek to gain admission to any watercloset forming part of such conveniences, and not being a watercloset set apart by the Council for use without payment, before any person who, by priority of payment of the sum charged by the Council as a fee for the use of such watercloset, shall be entitled to prior admission to such watercloset; or

(2.) enter, or seek to obtain entrance to any watercloset forming part of such conveniences, and being a watercloset set apart by the Council for use without payment, before any person desiring to use such watercloset, who, by priority of arrival, shall be entitled to the prior use of such watercloset.

Interfering with privacy.

4. A person using the sanitary conveniences shall not, by forcible or improper means, enter, or seek to gain admission to any closet or compartment forming part of such conveniences, which may, for the time being, be occupied by any other person, or otherwise knowingly intrude upon or interfere with the privacy of any other person who may be using such conveniences.

Improper use of conveniences.

5. A person using the sanitary conveniences shall not wilfully and improperly soil or defile any part of any staircase, floor, or passage, or of any wall, door, seat, or fitting, in the sanitary conveniences, or use any part of such conveniences for any purpose other than that for which it is constructed and intended to be used.

Male persons not to use women's conveniences, and *vice versâ*.

6. A person using the sanitary conveniences shall not, if a male, above the age of *seven years*, enter or intrude upon any part of such conveniences which may be set apart for the use of females, and shall not, if a female, enter or intrude upon any part of such conveniences which may be set apart for the use of males.

7. A person using the sanitary conveniences shall not on any part thereof cut, mark, write, or inscribe any word, letter, or figure, or post or affix any bill, placard, or advertisement: Writing on walls, posting bills, etc.

Provided always that this byelaw shall not apply to any act already punishable under any statutory provision in that behalf.

8. A person using the sanitary conveniences shall not make use of any indecent or obscene language to the annoyance of any other person using the sanitary conveniences, or cause any disturbance, or otherwise behave in an improper manner. Bad language and behaviour.

9. A person using the sanitary conveniences shall not carelessly or negligently break or injure, or improperly interfere with the due and efficient action of any lock, cock, valve, pipe, work, or other fitting in or in connection with such conveniences. Damage to, and improper interference with, fittings.

10. A person using the sanitary conveniences shall not occupy any watercloset for an unduly long time, and shall not, after using such conveniences, without reasonable excuse, loiter or remain in any part of such conveniences. Loitering and unreasonable use of waterclosets.

Penalties.

11. Every person who shall offend against any of the foregoing byelaws shall be liable for every such offence to a penalty of *forty shillings:* Penalties.

Provided, nevertheless, that the justices or court before whom any complaint may be made or any proceedings may be taken in respect of any such offence may, if they think fit, adjudge the payment, as a penalty, of any sum less than the full amount of the penalty imposed by this byelaw.

MANAGEMENT OF SANITARY CONVENIENCES.

REGULATIONS

MADE BY THE* WITH RESPECT TO THE MANAGEMENT OF THE PUBLIC SANITARY CONVENIENCES FOR† AT‡ .

Interpretation of terms.

Interpretation.

1. Throughout these regulations, the following words and expressions shall have the meanings hereinafter respectively assigned to them, that is to say,—

"Council" means the* ;

"Sanitary conveniences" means the sanitary conveniences for† provided and maintained by the Council for public accommodation, and situate at‡ ;

"Attendant" means the person for the time being appointed by the Council to take charge of the sanitary conveniences, or any part thereof.

With respect to the management of the sanitary conveniences.

Duties of attendant—Hours of attendance.

2.—(1.) The attendant shall be in attendance at the sanitary conveniences from o'clock in the morning until o'clock in the evening, of every day:

Inspection of conveniences.

(2.) *He* shall, before admitting any person to use the sanitary conveniences, ascertain by inspection that such conveniences, and all the fittings and appliances provided in, or in connection therewith, are in good order and condition, and ready for the use of the persons who may resort thereto:

Hours of opening and closing conveniences.

(3.) *He* shall cause the sanitary conveniences to be opened for public accommodation at o'clock in the morning, and to be closed to the public at o'clock in the evening, of every day:

---

* "Mayor, aldermen, and burgesses of the borough of , acting by the Council"; *or,* "Urban [*or* Rural] District Council of ," *as the case may be.*

† *Insert* "men," *or* "women," *or* "men and women," *as the case may require.*

‡ *The blank should be filled.*

(4.) *He* shall cause every part of the sanitary conveniences to be thoroughly cleansed on every day, before o'clock in the morning, and otherwise from time to time as often as occasion may require:

Cleansing of conveniences.

(5.) *He* shall cause the door of every watercloset forming part of the sanitary conveniences, when not required for use, to be kept locked:

Doors of waterclosets to be kept locked.

(6.) *He* shall comply with every reasonable requirement of any person using or desiring to use the sanitary conveniences:

Attention to persons using conveniences.

(7.) *He* shall take all lawful and proper measures to preserve order among the persons from time to time resorting to the sanitary conveniences, and to prevent any damage being done to such conveniences, or to any fitting or appliance provided in or in connection therewith:

Preservation of order, and prevention of damage.

(8.) *He* shall take due precautions to prevent waste or misuse of the water or gas supplied to the sanitary conveniences, and shall at the close of every day, before leaving the sanitary conveniences, cause all lights to be extinguished, and the water to be properly turned off:

Prevention of waste.

(9.) *He* shall, as soon as practicable after *he* shall have become aware of any breach of any byelaw or regulation for the time being in force as regards the sanitary conveniences or the decent conduct of persons using the same, or of any defect which may exist in such conveniences, or in any fitting or appliance provided in, or in connection therewith, report the facts of the case to the Council.

Reports to be made to Council.

CABMEN'S SHELTERS.

MEMORANDUM.

Authority for making the Byelaws and Regulations.

It is enacted by section 40 of the Public Health Acts Amendment Act, 1890 (53 & 54 Vict. c. 59), that,—

"(1.) An urban authority may from time to time provide, maintain, and remove in or near any street in their district suitable erections for the use, convenience, and shelter of drivers of hackney carriages, and such other persons as the urban authority may permit to use the same.

"(2.) The urban authority may from time to time make regulations for prescribing the terms and conditions and the fees (if any) to be charged for the use of such places of shelter, and may make byelaws for regulating the conduct of persons using the same."

Scope of the Model Byelaws and Regulations.

It will be noticed that the byelaws authorised by sub-section 2 of the above-cited enactment can only deal with the conduct of persons using the cabmen's shelters. The application of the term "conduct" does not seem to be necessarily limited to matters such as would be implied by the term "behaviour," and it has been construed in a wider sense than this in framing the annexed model byelaws: but the distinction between the conduct of persons using the cabmen's shelters and the terms and conditions on which they are to be permitted to use these erections must be carefully observed, as the bye-laws, like others authorised by the Public Health Acts, are enforceable by penalties, while no penalty can be attached to the infringement of the regulations referred to in the section. The enactment contemplates that permission to use the shelters may be given by the Local Authority to other persons besides the drivers of hackney carriages; and it would seem that if any such permission is given, the persons, other than hackney carriage drivers, who may use the shelters, may be defined by the regulations, if any, made under the section. The model byelaws and regulations assume that this course will be adopted.

Local Authorities competent to make Byelaws and Regulations.

Byelaws and regulations with respect to cabmen's shelters can only be made by an Urban District Council who have adopted Part III. of the Public Health Acts Amendment Act, 1890, in manner provided by section 3, or by a Rural District Council invested with the necessary powers by an order of the Local Government Board under section 5 of the Act.

Adoption of Byelaws and Regulations.

Both the byelaws and the regulations should be adopted under seal of the Local Authority, the sealing, in each case, being properly attested, and the actual date of sealing being inserted in the attestation.

Confirmation of the Byelaws.

Byelaws made by a District Council under section 40 of the Act of 1890 require confirmation by the Local Government Board, but not the regulations which may be made under that section. (See section 188 of the Public Health Act, 1875 (38 & 39 Vict. c. 55).) Where such byelaws are proposed to be made, they should be submitted to the Local Government Board, in the first instance, in draft.

Publication of the Regulations.

Any Local Authority making regulations under section 40 of the Act of 1890 above-mentioned may cause the regulations to be published in such manner as they see fit.

CABMEN'S SHELTERS.

BYELAWS

MADE BY THE* FOR REGULATING THE CONDUCT OF PERSONS USING CABMEN'S SHELTERS PROVIDED AND MAINTAINED BY THE SAID COUNCIL.

Interpretation of terms.

Interpretation of terms.

1. Throughout these byelaws the following words and expressions shall have the meanings hereinafter respectively assigned to them, that is to say,—

"Council" means* ;

"District" means† ;

"Cabmen's Shelter" means an erection provided or maintained by the Council, in or near any street in the district, for the use, convenience, and shelter of drivers of hackney carriages, and such other persons as, by any regulations made by them in that behalf, the Council may permit to use the same.

For regulating the conduct of persons using cabmen's shelters.

Bad language and behaviour.

2.—(1.) A person using a cabmen's shelter shall not, while in such shelter, use any indecent or obscene language to the annoyance of any other person using such shelter, or be guilty of any offensive, disorderly or improper conduct.

Misuse of shelters.

(2.) He shall not, in such shelter, light, trim, clean, or repair any lamp, or otherwise perform any act which may render any part of such shelter, or of any seat, table, or shelf therein, unfit for the shelter, use, or convenience of any other person who may be entitled to use such shelter.

Improper crowding.

(3.) He shall not, by forcible or improper means, seek admission to such shelter at any time when such shelter may

---

* "Mayor, aldermen, and burgesses of the borough of , acting by the Council"; *or,* "Urban [*or* Rural] District Council of ," *as the case may be.*

† *Insert name of borough or urban or rural district, or, if the byelaws are to apply to part only of a rural district,* "that portion of the Rural District of which comprises the contributory places of ," *as the case may be.*

be already occupied by the full number of persons entitled to use such shelter for whose use at one and the same time such shelter is conveniently adapted to be used.

(4.) He shall not carelessly or negligently break, or injure, or improperly interfere with any part of any lock or other fitting in such shelter, or carelessly or negligently injure or destroy, or wilfully, carelessly or negligently remove or displace any part of such shelter, or of any furniture or appliance therein. **Damage.**

(5.) He shall not carelessly or negligently injure or destroy any article supplied for use in such shelter, and shall in the use of such shelter and of every article or thing therein, exercise reasonable and proper care.

(6.) He shall not in any part of such shelter post or affix any bill, placard or paper. **Posting bills, etc.**

(7.) He shall not upon any part of such shelter, or of any furniture or fitting therein, cut, mark or inscribe any word, character, or figure. **Cutting and marking.**

Penalties.

3. Every person who shall offend against any of the foregoing byelaws, shall be liable for every such offence to a penalty of *forty shillings:* **Penalties.**

Provided, nevertheless, that the justices before whom any complaint may be made or any proceedings may be taken in respect of any such offence may, if they think fit, adjudge the payment, as a penalty, of any sum less than the full amount of the penalty imposed by this byelaw.

USER OF CABMEN'S SHELTERS.

REGULATIONS

MADE BY THE * FOR PRESCRIBING THE TERMS AND CONDITIONS, AND THE FEES (IF ANY) TO BE CHARGED FOR THE USE OF THE CABMEN'S SHELTERS PROVIDED AND MAINTAINED BY THE SAID COUNCIL.

Interpretation.

1. Throughout these regulations the following words and expressions shall have the meanings hereinafter respectively assigned to them, that is to say,—

"Council" means the* ;

"District" means the† ;

"Cabmen's Shelter" means an erection provided and maintained by the Council in or near any street in the district, for the use, convenience, and shelter of drivers of hackney carriages and other persons by these regulations permitted by the Council to use the same;

"Person entitled to use a cabmen's shelter" means any licensed driver of a hackney carriage, or any licensed driver or conductor of an omnibus, or any‡ .

Unauthorised persons not to be in shelter.

2. A person, not being a person entitled to use a cabmen's shelter, or a keeper of a coffee stall therein, or an officer or servant of the Council for the time being employed in the care and maintenance or inspection of cabmen's shelters, shall not enter or remain in any such shelter.

---

* Mayor, aldermen, and burgesses of the borough of , acting by the Council"; *or*, "Urban" *or* "Rural District Council of ," *as the case may be.*

† *Insert name of borough or urban or rural district, or, if the byelaws are to apply to part only of a rural district,* "that portion of the Rural District of which comprises the contributory places of ," *as the case may be.*

‡ *Here mention any other persons who are to be permitted to use the shelters.*

3. Every person using a cabmen's shelter in which there is a coffee stall, shall pay to the keeper of such stall, as a fee for the use of such shelter, a sum of *one penny* for *each day* on which such shelter shall be used by such person. Fee for use of shelter.

4. A person shall not use a cabmen's shelter except between * o'clock in the morning and* o'clock in the evening of any day. Hours.

5. A driver of a hackney carriage shall not, except in bad weather, use any cabmen's shelter at any time when his carriage shall be the first on the stand, in connection with which such shelter may have been provided. Hackney-carriage drivers.

6. A driver or conductor of an omnibus shall not use any cabmen's shelter at any time when his omnibus shall be standing or plying for hire. Omnibus drivers and conductors.

7. A † shall not use any cabmen's shelter at any time when‡ Other persons.

8. Every person using a cabmen's shelter shall, so far as he is able, assist in keeping such shelter in a cleanly and proper state. Keeping shelter clean, etc.

9. A person using a cabmen's shelter where there shall be no keeper of a coffee stall therein, shall, on it becoming known to him that any part of such shelter, or any lock or fitting, or any seat, table or shelf therein has been damaged or become unfit for use, report such damage or unfitness to the Council at their office. Damage.

---

* *Insert the hours.*

† *See note ‡ on previous page.*

‡ *Insert the conditions under which a cabmen's shelter may not be used by such persons.*

PART VIII.

ALLOTMENTS.

ALLOTMENTS PROVIDED BY COUNTY, BOROUGH, AND DISTRICT COUNCILS.

MEMORANDUM.

Authority for making Regulations.

Section 6 (1) of the Allotments Act, 1887 (50 & 51 Vict. c. 48), provides as follows :—

" Subject to the provisions of this Act, the sanitary authority may from time to time make, revoke, and vary such regulations as appear to be necessary or proper for regulating the letting of allotments under this Act, and for preventing any undue preference in the letting thereof, and generally for carrying the provisions of this Act into effect; and such regulations may define the persons eligible to be tenants of such allotments, and the notices to be given for the letting thereof, and the size of the allotments, and the conditions under which they are to be cultivated, and the rent to be paid for them. Provided that all such regulations shall make provision for reasonable notice to be given to a tenant of any allotment of the determination of his tenancy. Provided also, that all regulations made under this section shall not be of any force unless and until they have been confirmed by the Local Government Board, in like manner and subject to the like provisions as in the case of byelaws under the Public Health Act, 1875."

Local Authorities competent to make Regulations.

Regulations under section 6 (1) of the Allotments Act, 1887, may be made by the Council of any borough or other Urban District, or of any Rural District providing allotments under the Act. Under the Allotments Act, 1890 (53 & 54 Vict. c. 65), the council of an administrative county may also, in certain circumstances, make regulations under the enactment abovecited. (See sections 2 and 4 (*a*) of the Act of 1890, which, as regards rural parishes, should be read in connection with section 9 (14) of the Local Government Act, 1894 (56 & 57 Vict. c. 73).)

Scope of the Model Regulations.

The model regulations of the Local Government Board are strictly limited to matters mentioned in section 6 (1) of the Act of 1887. They do not, however, prescribe the rents to be paid for the allotments, as to which it is legally competent to Local Authorities to make regulations, the omission being no doubt due to the consideration that the rents may have to be varied from time to time. Matters as to which specific provision is made by statute, are also omitted. Thus there is nothing in the model series with regard to the sub-letting of allotments, or the conditions under which compensation is payable to a tenant on the determination of his tenancy, these matters being the subject of express enactment in sections 7 (3) and 8 (2) of the Allotments Act, 1887, and the Allotments and Cottage Gardens Compensation for Crops Act, 1887 (50 & 51 Vict. c. 26).

Persons eligible to be tenants of allotments.

The model regulation "for defining the persons eligible to be tenants of allotments" restricts eligibility to persons belonging to the "labouring population." It is for such persons only that the Local Authority are empowered to provide allotments (section 2 of the Allotments Act, 1887). The term "labouring population" is not defined in the Act, and cannot be defined in the regulations; but it may be taken to mean the population that, in substance, makes a livelihood by manual labour, including persons such as smiths, ploughmen, carpenters, artificers, workers in factories, and others whose work is chiefly manual, though it may require some knowledge and skill. It would seem, however, that the expression would not include persons whose work, though partly manual, is *mainly* a matter of knowledge and skill. Section 2 of the Allotments Act, 1887, however, does not prevent the letting of allotments to persons who, though they may "belong" to the labouring population, do not personally perform any manual labour, for example, the widow of a labourer.

Size of allotments.

In connection with clauses 2 and 5 of the model series, it may be pointed out that one person cannot hold *of the Council* any allotment or allotments exceeding *one acre* (section 7 (3) of the Allotments Act, 1887).

Register of allotments.

The reference in clause 3 of the model regulations is to section 15 of the Allotments Act, 1887.

Payment of rates and taxes by tenants.

No regulation on this subject is necessary in consequence of the provision in section 7 (2) of the Allotments Act, 1887.

Agreements for letting allotments.

The regulations being binding upon all persons whatsoever (section 6 (2) of the Allotments Act, 1887), it is not necessary to insert in the agreement for letting an allotment, a clause making the regulations part of the agreement. In case of non-observance of the regulations, the Council can, of course, give notice to the tenant determining his tenancy; and where not less than three months have elapsed after the commencement of the tenancy, the special provisions of section 8 (2) of the Act apply. The agreements cannot require payment of more than one quarter's rent in advance (section 7 (1) of the Act of 1887). If, however, the land is held for the purpose of allotments under any special conditions which it is thought desirable to expressly impose on the tenants of allotments, additional covenants for the purpose may be embodied in the form of agreement, or, if the special conditions directly affect the mode of cultivation, in clause 8 of the series. The agreements when executed, are subject to stamp duty.

Confirmation of regulations.

Regulations made by a county, borough, or district council under section 6 (1) of the Allotments Act, 1887, require confirmation by the Local Government Board. They should be submitted to that Board, in the first instance, in draft.

What is an "allotment."—A piece of ground less than two acres in extent, cultivated by a seedsman for the purpose of his trade, is not an allotment or cottage garden, and does not come within the Allotments and Cottage Gardens Compensation for Crops Act, 1887 (*Cooper* v. *Pearse*, [1896] 1 Q. B. 562; 60 J. P. 282; 65 L. J. M. C. 95; 74 L. T. 495; 44 W. R. 494).

MODEL REGULATIONS OF THE LOCAL GOVERNMENT BOARD AS TO ALLOTMENTS (COUNTY, BOROUGH, AND DISTRICT COUNCILS).

REGULATIONS

MADE BY THE * WITH RESPECT TO ALLOTMENTS FOR THE † .

Interpretation of terms.

1. Throughout these regulations the expression "the Council" means the* , or, if and so long as there are Allotment Managers who are empowered to carry out these regulations, such Managers; the expression "the District" means the‡ ; and the expression "the Parish" means§ .

For defining the persons eligible to be tenants of the allotments.

2. Any man or woman, of not less than twenty-one years of age, who at the time of application to the Council for an allotment has been resident in the‖ for not less than¶ months, and belongs to the labouring population, shall be eligible to become a tenant of an allotment.

Provided always, that a person who, at the time of such application, already holds an allotment, either from the Council or otherwise, shall not be eligible to become tenant of an allotment, the area of which, together with the area of any allotment or allotments already held by him, would amount to more than ** .

---

* "County Council for "; *or*, "Mayor, aldermen, and burgesses of the borough of , acting by the Council"; *or*, "Urban [*or* Rural] District Council of ," *as the case may be.*

† "Said borough"; *or*, "the Urban [*or* Rural] District *or* Parish of ," *as the case may be.*

‡ "Borough of "; *or*, "Urban [*or* Rural] District of ," *as the case may be.*

§ *Insert name of Parish. If, in a rural district, the allotments are provided for a contributory place which is not co-extensive with a poor law parish, the area should be described by the name of the contributory place.*

‖ "District" *or* "Parish."

¶ "Twelve months" *is suggested.*

** *See memorandum prefixed to this series.* "One acre" *might be inserted here.*

As to dividing the land into allotments.

3. The Council, before giving notice of their intention to let any allotment, shall divide the land, and shall cause a plan to be prepared showing each allotment, and distinguishing it by a separate number. They shall enter each allotment under its number in the register required to be kept, showing the particulars of the tenancy, acreage, and rent of every allotment.

The Council may from time to time re-divide any portion of the land. They shall enter and number each allotment formed on such re-division in the register in the manner herein-before described.

For defining the notices to be given for the letting of the allotments.

4. The Council shall give public notice by bills or placards, posted in some conspicuous places in the * or otherwise exhibited therein, setting forth the particulars as to any allotments which they propose to let.

Such notice shall specify the allotments to be let and the size thereof, the rent to be paid for the same, the place to which and the name of the person to whom application for the hiring of any allotment is to be sent, and the last day for receiving any such application.

For defining the size of the allotments.

5. The size of any allotment let by the Council shall not be less than† poles.

For regulating the letting of the allotments and preventing any undue preference in the letting thereof.

6. The Council shall not let any allotment unless and until notice that they propose to let the same has been duly given in pursuance of the regulation in that behalf‡ at least§ weeks before the last day for receiving applications to hire such allotment.

* "District" *or* "Parish."

† *It is suggested that* "twenty" *should be inserted here.*

‡ See clause 4.

§ "Two" *might be inserted.*

Every person who shall apply for an allotment shall furnish in the form hereto appended a true statement of the particulars therein required to be specified and shall send or deliver the same to the clerk to the Council, and it shall be the duty of such clerk to number the applications in the order in which they are received.

In letting an allotment for which there are two or more applicants eligible to become tenants, the Council shall select the applicant who appears most likely to keep the allotment in a proper state of cultivation; but in cases of equality in this respect the Council shall give preference to the applicants according to the order in which their applications are numbered as having been received.

Form of application for allotments.

To the* .

I the undersigned hereby make application for No. of the allotments provided for the† of .

1. Name .
2. Residence
3. Age .
4. Occupation .
5. How long resident in the† .
6. Whether holding any Allotment, and if so—
   (*a.*) From whom .
   (*b.*) Extent of Allotment

Signature

Date .

7. When the Council have decided to let any allotment or allotments to any person, an agreement shall be made between the Council and such person, and shall be signed by the clerk to the Council on behalf of the Council and by such person. The agreement shall be in the form hereinafter prescribed, or to the like effect.

---

* "Town Council for the Borough of "; *or*, "Urban [*or* Rural] District Council of "; *or*, "Allotment Managers for the of ," *as the case may be.*

† "Borough" *or* "District" *or* "Parish," *as the case may be.*

Form of agreement for letting.

Agreement made this day of 18 , between the (hereinafter called the Council) of the one part, and of (hereinafter called the tenant) of the other part, whereby the said Council agree to let, and the said tenant agrees to hire the allotment [or allotments] numbered in the register of allotments provided for the of , and containing or thereabouts, at the yearly rent of , and at a proportionate rent for any period of less than a year over which the tenancy may extend, subject to the following conditions:—

(*a.*) The rent shall be paid* on the day of , the day of , the day of , and the day of in each year.

(*b.*) Any member or officer of the Council shall be entitled at any time when directed by the Council to enter and inspect the allotment.

(*c.*) The tenancy, if not sooner terminated by the Council in pursuance of the Allotments Act, 1887, or of any Regulations made thereunder, shall terminate on the death of the tenant, or after months' notice in writing given by the tenant, such notice to expire on the or .

Signed

Clerk to the

Witness .

Signed

Tenant.

Witness

For defining the conditions under which the allotments are to be cultivated.

8. Every person to whom an allotment may have been let shall cultivate such allotment according to the following conditions, that is to say:—

He shall keep the allotment free from weeds, and well manured, and otherwise maintain it in a proper state of cultivation;

He shall not plant any trees or shrubs so as to be injurious to any adjacent allotment;

He shall keep every hedge that shall form part of the allotment properly cut and trimmed;

---

* *Insert* "in advance" *if this is intended.*

He shall not cause any nuisance or annoyance to the tenant of any other allotment.

As to the reasonable notice to be given to a tenant of any allotment of the determination of his tenancy.

9. The Council shall give to the tenant of any allotment not less than month's notice of the determination of his tenancy, such notice to take effect on or .

Provided always that this regulation shall not apply in the case of the determination of a tenancy in pursuance of the statutory provision in that behalf, where the rent is in arrear for not less than forty days, or where it appears to the Council that the tenant of an allotment, not less than three months after the commencement of the tenancy thereof, has not duly observed the regulations affecting such allotment, or is resident more than one mile out of the* . .

For prescribing the manner in which the register of allotments shall be open to the examination of ratepayers.

10. The register showing the particulars of the tenancy, acreage, and rent of every allotment let, and of the unlet allotments, shall be deposited at the office of the , and shall be open during office hours to the examination of any ratepayer in the* .

* "District" *or* "Parish."

ALLOTMENTS PROVIDED BY PARISH COUNCILS.

MEMORANDUM

of the Local Government Board with respect to Allotment Regulations for Parish Councils.

Authority for making regulations.

1. Under sub-section (1) of section 6 of the Allotments Act, 1887,* which applies to allotments hired by or vested in a Parish Council under the Local Government Act, 1894,† a Parish Council may make regulations with respect to the letting of such allotments, for preventing any undue preference in the letting thereof, and generally as to the carrying into effect of the provisions of the Act of 1887 so far as they apply to such allotments. The regulations may define the persons eligible to be tenants of the allotments, the notices to be given for the letting of them, the size of the allotments and the conditions under which they are to be cultivated. They are to make provision for reasonable notice being given to a tenant of the determination of his tenancy.

Confirmation of regulations.

2. Before such regulations can take effect they require confirmation by the Local Government Board in like manner and subject to the like provisions as in the case of byelaws under the Public Health Act, 1875.

Use of model forms.

3. The Board have prepared a model series of regulations for the use of Parish Councils in framing regulations under the Act of 1887 as to allotments of arable land. Any regulations proposed to be made by a Parish Council should be submitted to the Board in draft on one of their model forms for their preliminary approval, before any steps are taken for the formal adoption of the regulations.

4. Any clauses in addition to or in substitution for those of the model series should be inserted in the draft on separate sheets

---

* 50 & 51 Vict. c. 48.

† 56 & 57 Vict. c. 73.

of paper with half margin; minor alterations may conveniently be shown in the margin of the model form.

Scope of regulations.

5. The regulations should not include matters as to which specific provision is made by statute: for instance, they should not deal with the sub-letting of allotments, as section 7 (3) of the Act of 1887 expressly prohibits sub-letting.

Information to be furnished.

6. When the draft regulations are forwarded to the Board for approval, the following information should be furnished:—

(1.) The area of the land acquired for allotments.

(2.) Whether the land was purchased by the County Council and assured to the Parish Council under sub-section (14) of section 9 of the Local Government Act, 1894; or

(3.) Whether the land was hired by the Parish Council under section 10 of the Act of 1894; and

(4.) Whether the land is all arable, or whether it includes pasture, and, if so, what proportion of the land is pasture.

Lease or agreement.

7. A copy of any lease or agreement under which the land is held by the Parish Council should likewise be sent to the Board. It will be returned.

Allotments to which regulations may apply.

Making of regulations not obligatory.

8. The power to make the regulations above referred to will only apply to allotments held by the Parish Council under either section 9 (14) or section 10 of the Local Government Act, 1894. It is not obligatory on a Parish Council to make regulations. Without regulations they can enter into an agreement with the proposed tenant of any allotment, and the agreement may contain such stipulations as the circumstances of the case require.

LOCAL GOVERNMENT BOARD,
November, 1897.

MODEL REGULATIONS OF THE LOCAL GOVERNMENT BOARD AS TO ALLOTMENTS OF ARABLE LAND (PARISH COUNCILS).

REGULATIONS

MADE BY THE PARISH COUNCIL OF THE PARISH OF WITH RESPECT TO ALLOTMENTS FOR THE SAID PARISH.

Regulations.—These regulations are not enforceable by penalties, but are binding on all persons whatsoever (s. 6 (2) of the Allotments Act, 1887 ; see also s. 8 (2) of the same Act).

Interpretation of terms.

1. Throughout these regulations the expression "the Council" means the Parish Council of the Parish of ; and the expression "the Parish" means the Parish of .

For defining the persons eligible to be tenants of the allotments.

2. Any man or woman, of not less than twenty-one years of age, who at the time of application to the Council for an allotment has been resident in the Parish for not less than months,* and belongs to the labouring population, shall be eligible to become a tenant of an allotment.

Provided always, that a person who, at the time of such application, already holds an allotment, either from the Council or otherwise, shall not be eligible to become tenant of an allotment, the area of which, together with the area of any allotment or allotments already held by him, would amount to more than † .

Persons eligible to be tenants.—The allotments can be held only by persons belonging to the labouring population (s. 2 (1) of the Allotments Act, 1887). The term "labouring population" is not defined in the Act, and cannot be defined by the regulations. The expression, however, would include all persons whose work is chiefly, if not entirely, manual, though it may require some knowledge and skill. On the other hand, persons whose work,

* "Twelve months" *is suggested.*

† A reasonable amount should be specified.

though partly manual, is mainly a matter of skill and knowledge, would not be included in the term. It may be said, then, that persons such as smiths, ploughmen, and artificers belong to the labouring population, but that cooks, nurses, clerks, and tradesmen generally, do not. A person not actually labouring, may nevertheless "belong" to the labouring population, *e.g.*, the widow of a labourer.

As to dividing the land into allotments and keeping a register of allotments.

3. The Council, before giving notice of their intention to let any allotment, shall divide the land, and shall cause a plan to be prepared showing each allotment, and distinguishing it by a separate number. They shall enter each allotment under its number in a register which shall be kept by them, showing the particulars of the tenancy, acreage, and rent of every allotment.

The Council may from time to time re-divide any portion of the land. They shall number each allotment formed on such re-division and enter it in the register in the manner herein-before prescribed.

Register of allotments.—Section 15 of the Allotments Act, 1887, which relates to the keeping of a register of allotments, does not apply to a Parish Council. It is, however, very desirable that such a register should be kept, and this regulation will require it to be done.

For defining the notices to be given for the letting of the allotments.

4. The Council shall give public notice in the manner required by section 51 of the Local Government Act, 1894, of the particulars as to any allotments which they propose to let.

Such notice shall specify the allotments to be let and the size thereof, the rent to be paid for the same, the name and address of the Clerk of the Council to whom application for the hiring of any allotment is to be sent, and the last day for receiving any such application.

Giving of notices.—Section 51 of the Local Government Act, 1894, provides that "a public notice given by a parish council for the purposes of this Act, or otherwise for the execution of their duties . . . shall be given in the manner required for giving notice of vestry meetings, and by posting the notice in some conspicuous place or places within the parish, and in such other manner (if any) as appears to the council . . . desirable for giving publicity to the notice."

For defining the size of the allotments.

5. The size of any allotment let by the Council shall not be less than poles, nor more than * .

For regulating the letting of the allotments and preventing any undue preference in the letting thereof.

6. The Council shall not let any allotment unless and until notice that they propose to let the same has been duly given in pursuance of the regulation in that behalf† at least‡ weeks before the last day for receiving applications to hire such allotment.

Every person who shall apply for an allotment shall submit his application in writing. § He shall state therein the number of such allotment in the register kept by the Council, and furnish a true statement of the following particulars; that is to say,—

1. His christian name and surname:
2. His place of residence:
3. His age:
4. His occupation:
5. How long he has been resident in the parish:
6. Whether he holds any allotment, and if so—
   (*a.*) From whom;
   (*b.*) The extent of the allotment.

He shall date and sign the application, and shall send or deliver the same to the Clerk of the Council.

All such applications shall be numbered by the Clerk of the Council in the order in which they are received.

In letting an allotment for which there are two or more applicants eligible to become tenants, the Council shall select the applicant who appears most likely to keep the allotment in a proper state of cultivation; but in cases of equality in this respect the Council shall give preference to the applicants

---

* If the land has been hired compulsorily, the size of an allotment consisting of arable land must not exceed one acre. See section 10 (6) (*a*) of the Local Government Act, 1894.

† See clause 4.

‡ "Two" *might be inserted.*

§ No special form will be required, but the application must contain the information specified.

according to the order in which their applications are numbered as having been received.

7. When the Council have decided to let any allotment or allotments to any person, an agreement shall be made between the Council and such person, in the form hereinafter prescribed, or in a form to the like effect.

Form of agreement for letting.

Agreement made this day of 18 , between the Parish Council of the parish of (hereinafter called the Council) of the one part, and of (hereinafter called the tenant) of the other part, whereby the Council agree to let, and the tenant agrees to hire the allotment [*or* allotments] numbered in the register of allotments provided for the Parish, and containing or thereabouts, at the yearly rent of* , and at a proportionate rent for any period of less than a year over which the tenancy may extend, subject to the following conditions:—

(*a.*) The rent shall be paid† on the day of , the day of , the day of , and the day of in each year.‡

(*b.*) Any member or officer of the Council shall be entitled at any time when directed by the Council to enter and inspect the allotment.

(*c.*) The tenant shall be at liberty to erect on the allotment a stable, cowhouse, or barn.§

(*d.*) The tenancy, if not sooner terminated by the Council in pursuance of the Local Government Act, 1894, and the

---

* This space should be left blank in the regulations. It is undesirable to fix the rents by means of a regulation, as they may have to be varied from time to time. No regulation is necessary as regards the payment of rates and taxes by the tenant (see s. 7 (2) of the Allotments Act, 1887).

† *Insert* "in advance" *if this is intended.*

‡ Not more than one quarter's rent can be required to be paid in advance (s. 7 (1) of the Allotments Act, 1887).

§ This clause is no doubt inserted in consequence of the provision in s. 10 (6) (*b*) of the Local Government Act, 1894. No provision in the agreement is necessary to enable the tenant (in the absence of any express prohibition under the terms of his holding) to erect on the allotment any toolhouse, shed, greenhouse, fowl-house, or pigstye (s. 7 (5) of the Allotments Act, 1887). But it would appear that, where necessary, the Council could, by a clause in the agreement, forbid the erection of any building on the allotment, except with their previous consent in writing.

Allotments Act, 1887, or of any Regulations made thereunder, shall terminate on the death of the tenant, or after months' notice in writing given by the tenant, such notice to expire on the* or .†

Signed

Chairman.‡

Witness

Parish Councillors.

Signed

Tenant.

Witness

For defining the conditions under which the allotments are to be cultivated.

8. Every person to whom an allotment may have been let shall cultivate such allotment according to the following conditions, that is to say:—

He shall keep the allotment free from weeds, and well manured, and otherwise maintain it in a proper state of cultivation;

He shall not plant any trees or shrubs so as to be injurious to any adjacent allotment;

He shall not cause any nuisance or annoyance to the tenant of any other allotment.

As to the reasonable notice to be given to a tenant of any allotment of the determination of his tenancy.

9. The Council shall give to the tenant of any allotment not less than months' notice of the determination of his tenancy, such notice to take effect on or .

Provided always that this regulation shall not apply in the case of the determination of a tenancy in pursuance of the

* As to the "reasonable notice" to be given by the Council to determine the tenancy of an allotment holder, see clause 9.

† With regard to the conditions under which compensation will be payable to the tenant on the determination of his tenancy, see s. 8 (2) of the Allotments Act, 1887, and the provisions of the Allotments and Cottage Gardens (Compensation for Crops) Act, 1887 (50 & 51 Vict. c. 26).

‡ The agreement should be signed at a meeting of the Council by the chairman of the meeting and two councillors.

statutory provision in that behalf,* where the rent is in arrear for not less than forty days, or where it appears to the Council that the tenant of an allotment, not less than three months after the commencement of the tenancy thereof, has not duly observed the regulations affecting such allotment, or is resident more than one mile out of the parish.

For prescribing the manner in which the register of allotments required by these regulations to be kept by the Council shall be open to examination.

10. The register to be kept by the Council in pursuance of these regulations shall be deposited with the clerk of the Council, and shall be open between the hours of† on *any day other than Sunday* to the examination of any parochial elector in the parish.

‡GIVEN under our hands and seals, at a meeting of the Parish Council held after due notice thereof this day of 18 .

(L.S.)
Presiding Chairman at the said Meeting.
(L.S.)
(L.S.)
Two Members of the Parish Council.

---

* See s. 8 (2) of the Allotments Act, 1887. No attempt should be made to vary the terms of this proviso.

† Insert the hours.

‡ This form of attestation is suggested by the Editors. Section 3 (9) of the Local Government Act, 1894, taken in connection with s. 182 of the Public Health Act, 1875, requires that the byelaws shall be signed by the chairman presiding at a meeting of the Parish Council and two other members of the Council, and that each of the persons signing shall affix his seal. A wafer seal, or any other kind o seal that may be convenient, may be adopted for the purpose. But there should be a separate seal in connection with each signature, and there should be no reference to any seal as the seal of the Parish Council. The Council, as a body, are not entitled to use a seal.

INDEX.

INDEX.

A.

B.

C.

D.

E.

F.

G.

H.

I.

J.

L.

M.

* The letters "(L. G. B.)" indicate that the model byelaws, etc., are those of the Local Government Board.

N.

O.

S.

T.

U.

V.

PRINTED BY SHAW AND SONS, FETTER LANE AND CRANE COURT, E.C.

www.ingramcontent.com/pod-product-compliance
Lightning Source LLC
Chambersburg PA
CBHW030314270326
41926CB00010B/1353

9783337157586